Praise for

When Mary Calls

"Margarita Mooney Clayton reminds us of something the modern world has almost forgotten: that Mary is not a sectarian figure but the mother of ALL who follow Christ—Pentecostal, Orthodox, and Catholic. This remarkable book rekindles our sense of wonder at the mysterious partnership between the human and the divine. It invites readers to rediscover a faith in which heaven touches earth, and miracles lead us deeper into truth. *When Mary Calls* is essential reading."

—**Eric Metaxas,** #1 *New York Times* bestselling author of *Bonhoeffer: Pastor, Martyr, Prophet, Spy* and host of *Socrates in the City* and *The Eric Metaxas Show*

"An encounter with Mary is unexpected in our time—because she's almost universally misunderstood. Dr. Margarita Mooney Clayton traces the many ways over that wall of misunderstanding. First among them is Scripture, of course, and the beauty of biblical typology. I love this book."

—**Dr. Scott Hahn,** the Father Michael Scanlan TOR Professor of Biblical Theology and the New Evangelization at Franciscan University of Steubenville and author of *Hail Holy Queen: The Mother of God in the Word of God*

"As the shadow of secularism passes over us, an increasing multitude of people wish to experience a deep connection with God and experience His presence in creation. *When Mary Calls* will help us remember Mary as both the Mother of God and our own mother. Margarita Mooney Clayton shows us the many ways Mary guides us to the embodiment of her Son."

—**Jonathan Pageau**, icon carver, public speaker, YouTuber, editor of the *Orthodox Arts Journal*, and host of *The Symbolic World* blog and podcast

"In a series of penetrating case studies and interviews, Margarita Mooney Clayton brings alive the dynamic presence of the Virgin Mary in the lives of contemporary persons—Christians of various denominations as well as non-Christians, men and women of widely different backgrounds and situations. To read *When Mary Calls* is to stumble unexpectedly upon an ancient healing well hidden in the folds of our dry modern world."

—**Dr. Peter Brown**, the Philip and Beulah Rollins Professor of History, Emeritus, at Princeton University and author of *Augustine of Hippo: A Biography*

"As someone who learned gradually to befriend and love the Blessed Mother, these stories resonated with my own experience. Mary is truly our patient mother. I once claimed I did not need Mary, but she still quietly revealed herself to me in providential and miraculous ways. This journey led me closer to Christ because Mary always leads us closer to Christ. May these stories deepen your appreciation for Our Lady's maternal role in your life."

—**Fr. Lawrence Lew, O.P.**, Promotor Generalis pro Rosario (Global Promoter of the rosary for the Dominican Order) and author of *Mysteries Made Visible: Praying the Rosary with Sacred Art*

When Mary Calls

SURPRISING ENCOUNTERS WITH THE MOTHER OF GOD

Margarita Mooney Clayton

ODYSSEUS BOOKS

For my mother, Eulalia (Lala) Maria Suarez de Mooney,
whose compassion knows no bounds

Odysseus books may be purchased in bulk at special discounts for sales promotion, corporate gifts, fund-raising, or educational purposes. Special editions can also be created to specifications. For details, contact the Special Sales Department, Skyhorse Publishing, 307 Fifth Avenue, 4th Floor, New York, NY 10016 or info@skyhorsepublishing.com.

Odysseus Books® is an imprint of Skyhorse Publishing, Inc.®, a Delaware corporation.

Visit our website at www.skyhorsepublishing.com.
Please follow our publisher Tony Lyons on Instagram
@tonylyonsisuncertain.

10 9 8 7 6 5 4 3 2 1

Library of Congress Cataloging-in-Publication Data is available on file.

Cover design by David Ter-Avanesyan
Cover image by David Clayton

Print ISBN: 978-1-63144-092-2
Ebook ISBN: 978-1-63144-093-9

Printed in the United States of America

Contents

Foreword

So many people in the world today are confused about what it means to be a person and to be a mother. Feminism, digital isolation, broken families, psychological pain, and fragmentation of all kinds have left many people cynical that life can be anything more than an endless competition or a series of pointless struggles.

That's why *When Mary Calls* is such an important book. It's a fresh look at how Mary, the Mother of God, is touching people's lives today in unexpected ways. When I first met Margarita, I enthusiastically offered to share how Mary led me to faith and the church. Each person's story in this book—including mine—brings to light how God's grace is always at work in the world, even when we have trouble seeing it. As she did with me when she came to my home for several days in 2024, Margarita reveals how Mary's motherhood has helped her in spiritual battles.

In each story, my friend Margarita captures the unique character of a person discerning God's calls in his or her life. She enlightens their spiritual journeys with her reflections on sacred art and music, as well as with her expertise in theology, philosophy, and sociology.

The Scriptures are at heart a book of wisdom. Each person's story in this book reveals that wisdom in powerful, personal ways.

Most importantly, the Mother of our Lord, who is too often forgotten, is powerfully present in these pages. You will read about various ways Mary touches people, heals them, and carries them to God. This book will help you know that Mary is calling you, too.

Mary is revered by so many throughout time and place because she teaches us to have courage to say "yes" to God, even when it's scary. This book is Margarita's "yes": a deep, compelling, courageous answer to God's invitation to be used for his purposes. I trust that through God's great mercy, *When Mary Calls* will bring forth great fruit for the world, just as Mary did.

—Tammy Peterson resides in Toronto, Ontario, Canada
October 17, 2025

INTRODUCTION

The Modern Quest for Mary

A "Wild Marian Experience"

One night in 2023, I woke up to a text from a fervent Christian raised in the Bible Belt named Evan.[1]

"Margarita, I had a wild Marian experience!"

In the darkness of my room, I saw on my phone what appeared to be an image of Mary.

I wondered: Why was Evan, a Protestant who had never mentioned Mary to me in our decade-long friendship, suddenly writing to me about an encounter with her?

During a phone call not long after that text message, Evan explained how, during a hiking trip that took him to several European countries, he set out for the cliffs in southwest Ireland known as the Skellig Islands. Familiar to some as a film location for the Star Wars films and the site of monastery founded in the sixth century, those islands sparked Evan's imagination, since he had always been an enthusiast of ancient history. The fog surrounding the island added to its mystique.

While mapping his route through that area of Ireland, the app on his phone indicated a spot labeled as a healing well. Evan felt completely worn out from his travels; in particular, his throat was swollen. Out of curiosity, he stopped at the healing well. He sent me a picture of a statue of Mary dressed in blue and white at the well, with rosaries dangling from her arms and a prayer inscribed on a plaque.

As if wanting to recall that powerful moment, he read the prayer out loud to me over the phone:

> May our Lady bless you in your going, your coming, and your staying;
> may she bless you in your thinking, your doing, and your saying;
> may she bless you in your joys and bless you when you weep;
> may she bless you in your waking and bless you when you sleep;
> may she keep her arms around you and fold you to her heart,
> till you meet with her and Jesus where you never more will part. Amen.

What happened next was so unexpected that Evan has been pondering it in his heart ever since. "I felt compelled to kneel and wash my face in the water. When I did, I immediately sensed the sickness draining from my body." He insisted that he didn't think much about what he was doing; he just followed his instincts in reciting the prayer and washing himself. The physical healing was accompanied by a profound spiritual encounter, which Evan described as "an enveloping sense of warmth, serenity, and peace." And then he added, "I just felt a tremendous sense of intimacy with God and gratitude for my spiritual mother."

Embodied Religion, Marian Pilgrimages, and a New Pentecost

Evan's experience, and the other unexpected encounters with Mary I share in this book, reflect a larger trend: growing interest in Mary in popular culture and religious communities that have not historically practiced devotion to her, such as by asking for her blessing, which Evan did when he recited the prayer at the well. Evan's willingness to stop at a Marian shrine and speak to Mary as his spiritual mother is part of an opening among many Evangelical and Mainline Protestants to the kinds of embodied experiences of faith—such as prayers to Mary—that once characterized nearly all of Christianity.

Why, in this so-called secular age of disenchantment, are people across denominational lines, or with little or no religious background, seeking a relationship with Mary? Mary's motherhood of the faithful has historically been understood as leading people more deeply into the communion of the church. In our era of individualistic faith, a relationship with Mary offers interior spiritual renewal for believers like Evan that binds him more to the community of the church, past and present.

Our secular, disenchanted culture has been several centuries in the making. As moral philosopher Alasdair MacIntyre argued in his landmark book *After Virtue* (1981), eighteenth-century Enlightenment philosophers portrayed man as rational, utilitarian, and essentially self-seeking. For those philosophers and their modern heirs, "autonomy," the free choice to make your life whatever you want it to be, was the supreme goal. Any form of dependence, including dependence on a creator God, was deemed a barrier to freedom.

The result was a materialist erosion of faith in God that accelerated into the twentieth century. By the time I was born in 1973, fewer people in the United States and most of Europe attended church, believed in Christian creeds or moral doctrines, or sought ultimate meaning in a transcendent God. Increasingly, we saw the cost of these changes: people felt alone, spiritually adrift, and alienated from genuine community. Faith, where it continued, was often thought of in individualistic terms, not as flowing from the living water of a church community.

But by the end of the twentieth century, signs emerged that secularization and individualistic faith could be slowing or even reversing. In much of Europe, the continent's Catholic pilgrimage sites like Lourdes in France and Fátima in Portugal—where Marian apparitions and miracles were observed in 1858 and 1917, respectively—saw an increase in visitors in the first two decades of the twenty-first century. Although it's difficult to know precisely the demographic and religious composition of the pilgrims to Marian shrines in Europe, the estimated four million annual visitors to Lourdes and six million annual visitors to Fátima undoubtedly include more than practicing Catholics. One observer noted that pilgrimage sites across Protestant Europe that were once abandoned after the Reformation are being revived, such as in Norway.[2] Kneeling down, washing oneself, lighting candles, and asking for Mary's intercession are practices no longer just for Catholics.

People from a wide variety of backgrounds are looking to Mary as they seek to discern the presence of the Holy Spirit and the coming of a new fire of Pentecost to arise from the ashes of cultural confusion. While Mary's presence at the Incarnation and the crucifixion is well known, her role at Pentecost is often overlooked. Her name does not appear in the dramatic narrative of the coming of the Holy Spirit in Acts 2:1–4, but Acts 1:14 powerfully affirms her presence in the upper room just a few verses earlier: "All these with one accord devoted themselves to prayer, together with the women and Mary the mother of Jesus, and with his brethren."

Life with the Spirit bestows freedom: we are children of God who relate to him through love. Picturing Mary at Pentecost, recalling the coming of the Holy Spirit upon the early church, reminds us that that the blessed life we desire is life in the Spirit.

We need this same Pentecostal fire to rise from the ashes of our cultural confusion. At a time when many people are staring into the abyss with fear, Mary is appearing in unexpected places, drawing seekers from all backgrounds into the living community of faith. Countless people experience her closeness to them as the first disciples of Christ undoubtedly did. Mary embodies the fruits of the Spirit—love, joy, peace, patience, kindness, goodness, faithfulness, gentleness, and self-control (see Galatians 5:22–26). A relationship with her leads us, too, from servile fear to spiritual freedom.

People today seek more than bland spirituality disconnected from the body of the church and living tradition. They want Pentecostal moments. But after those life-changing experiences of grace, or those mystical movements in the soul, how do we connect our inner lives to the church? Mary's cooperation with God's grace reminds us that we, too, can transform peak spiritual moments into sustained practice, leading us from division to unity, fear to courage, confusion to light. Because Mary binds people to authentic faith community, she is a guardrail against individualistic spirituality detached from tradition and a life of service to others. Most people do not reason their way to faith but come to faith through relationships. As Mary well knew, living a life led by God's grace also does not mean we can abandon our human nature, our bodies, nor our intellect in a merely spiritual search for God.

God sent his son Jesus as our Redeemer, and Jesus left us his mother as our spiritual mother. Remembering Mary's motherhood of the faithful is not somehow saying Christ's saving work is insufficient for our redemption. Rather, God calls to each of us to collaborate freely and completely with him in that work. When we give the best of ourselves to collaborate with God, as Mary did, it is Christ's power and mercy that are glorified.

Pondering Mary's motherhood strengthens the call to self-sacrificial love in our own lives, whether that be in marriage and childrearing or giving ourselves in service to those around us, as she undoubtedly did. As the Mother of Christ, Mary's cooperation with him is unique. But in his love for us, Jesus wants to share the close relationship he had with his mother.

The stories recorded in this book illustrate that Mary's spiritual motherhood is available to all, regardless of our personal circumstances, drawing us into the family of God and into a deep intimacy with the Trinity, which is the ultimate source of human happiness. Evan's experience of Mary's spiritual motherhood led him into greater intimacy with God. Her motherhood does not belong to just one person, period, culture, or group within the church. She's the mother of all the faithful, calling us each to a closer relationship with all three persons of the Trinity.

Mary Is the Mother of All Christians—Protestant, Orthodox, and Catholic

Hardly a week goes by when I do not see another article about Mary's enduring appeal in unexpected places. Flagship publications in the Protestant world, such as *Christianity Today*, *Comment*, and *Christian Scholars Review*, have all recently featured important pieces of theological scholarship and personal reflections on Mary. Given that one of the effects of the Reformation was to remove Mary from much reflection on dogmatic theology and from the prayer life of the faithful, this Protestant attention to Mary is quite surprising.

For example, Matthew Milliner, a professor at the prestigious midwestern Evangelical school Wheaton College, has produced extensive scholarship on art history and Christianity that includes books and articles on Mary. In a 2023 essay for *Comment*, a magazine that reaches thoughtful readers across the Protestant world and engages with Catholic and Orthodox authors and readers as well, Milliner stated that

Mary "keeps showing up where she is supposed to be absent." Love for Mary does not detract from Jesus, Milliner insists, as love is not a zero-sum game. Quoting often-forgotten teachings about Mary from reformers like Martin Luther and John Calvin, Milliner argues that Mary should be everybody's mother today—Protestant, Catholic, and Orthodox—because Mary "is a safeguard against the mysticism that either forgets grace by carving out our own path to God or neglects the importance of the physical body."[3]

Embodied religious practices like pilgrimages offer disenchanted Christians and scientific rationalists something they are not getting elsewhere: a way of following God that recognizes the importance of human embodiment without discounting the intellect and the truth. A relationship with Mary enacted by asking for her motherly intercessions—often thought of as a barrier to ecumenical prayer since the Reformation—now offers a glimpse of Christian unity across denominations. For example, Our Lady of Walsingham in southern England marks an eleventh-century vision of Mary that has been revived as an ecumenical pilgrimage site. Once a popular destination for medieval Catholic pilgrims, the site was demolished during the English Reformation. King Henry VIII's 1538 injunction, given by Thomas Cromwell, an English statesman and lawyer who served the king, commanded the king's subjects "not to repose their trust and affiance in any other works devised by men's phantasies besides Scripture; as in wandering to pilgrimages, offering of money, candles, or tapers to images or relics, or kissing or licking the same, saying over a number of beads, not understood or minded on, or in such-like superstition."[4]

One noted Catholic journalist in England, Kevin Turley, described the unique nature of Our Lady of Walsingham's return to popularity: today it is an ecumenical pilgrimage site where Catholic, Anglican, Orthodox, and Reformed pilgrims each arrive carrying their own banners and Bibles. Although the tensions and divisions persist, he remarked on the inspiration he mysteriously felt as he awaited a new Pentecost: he joined his "separated brethren . . . in the Upper Room, all gathered around their spiritual mother, praying for unity" (Acts 1:14).[5]

Encountering Mary Through the Fine Arts

Mary's appeal extends into the fine arts. As Mary has been the object of so much cultural creativity across millennia, it's not surprising to see her represented in art exhibitions. But I am nonetheless pleasantly surprised when I see a museum—an ostensibly secular space—presenting a theological rendition of Mary's relationships with the faithful who have created that art and venerated those images as sacred objects that stimulate an intimate encounter with God through prayer. For example, in 2015, the National Museum of Women in the Arts in Washington, DC, devised an historical exposition of sixty mostly European medieval paintings of Mary as part of a program "to examine humanist themes related to womankind."[6]

Reading about this exhibition, I was struck by how, rather than reimagining Mary through modern secular lenses of worldly power, the paintings chosen by the museum's curators seemed to be faithful to how Christians have honored Mary for her spiritual motherhood throughout history. I failed to see what I often have observed in art galleries: an attempt to apologize for images that portray Mary's motherhood in traditional terms of nurturing and healing, as if such images would supposedly illustrate the subservient place of women in Christianity.

In fact, the organization of the exhibition resembled the major themes the eminent historian of Christianity Jaroslav Pelikan uses to organize his book, *Mary Through the Centuries: Her Place in the History of Culture* (1996). For example, the exhibition's themes included friendship, explored through Mary's intimacy with her cousin Elizabeth and her marriage with Joseph. The exhibition also included images of Mary at the foot of the cross, images understood as symbolizing supernatural hope in the face of injustice. Interestingly, even in a secular space like this museum, the exhibition featured Mary as she has been understood in Christian doctrine: as a bridge leading the faithful to her son Jesus. Mary was further portrayed as a gateway between heaven and earth and as symbolizing the promised return to the new Garden of Eden.

To accompany the in-person exhibition, an online exhibition was developed that is called "A Global Icon: Mary in Context."[7] From tapestries to statues, church ceilings and wall frescos, medallions and private devotional books, from every continent and all ages of Christianity, this rich pictorial and video exhibition presented a thoughtful glimpse into why Mary is, as Pelikan calls her, a woman for all times and all places.

Exhibitions such as this can inspire artists today to heed the call to co-create with God. As we will see later in this book, Christians in the arts encounter Mary not just as an object or an historical artifact, but as a subject, a living force, inspiring their creativity and directing their talents towards a cultural and civilizational renewal.

Mary's Spiritual Motherhood in an Era of Global Population Decline

For a long time, even as my personal relationship with Mary as my spiritual mother grew, I eschewed speaking about Mary in public lest I somehow sadden those women who—by choice or by circumstance—may not have biological children of their own. More recently, I have begun speaking publicly about Mary's motherhood of God because it reminds us that Christianity is a family, whether we are single or married, with or without children.

Nicholas Eberstadt, a political economist at the American Enterprise Institute (AEI), has shown that most parts of the world, not only the wealthier countries of the West, are presently undergoing a population decline. Around the globe from India to Mexico to Turkey and beyond, people are having fewer children, and many people will have no children.[8] Sociologist W. Bradford Wilcox of the University of Virginia estimates that one-third of young adults in America will never get married. Despite the claim that marriage and family are burdens, Wilcox argues that the social science data overwhelmingly points to marriage and family as sources of meaning, purpose, and fulfillment.[9]

I was unmarried until the age of forty-eight. Although now I have wonderful stepchildren, I never had the biological children I desired and often felt unworthy because of that. Thus, I cannot help but note the longing for intimate family ties among people in similar positions as I was. When my desire for marriage did not materialize as a young woman, I was encouraged to pursue my career, and I am glad I did. But I needed more than achievements and economic independence to be happy. The community of faith became like an extended family, where I experienced deep friendships—a great gift of love and intimacy fortified by a shared journey toward God. Regardless of our personal situation, Mary's motherhood pulls all of us into the spiritual family of the church.

Knowing Mary Through Stories: How to Read This Book

Each chapter in this book recounts a different person's close relationship with Mary. Together, I hope these experiences present a tapestry of deeply personal, testimonial-style stories of Marian encounters. Her presence is found in these stories through a moment of miraculous intervention, a moment of great creative inspiration, or a moment of life-changing grace that leads to a new vision. Each chapter presents one person's testimony of Mary alive in his or her life today; we see each person searching the Scriptures, looking inside their hearts, looking to tradition and history and attempting to understand the movement of God in their lives, which they discern through Mary's presence.

Each story is a kind of spiritual memoir, capturing the inner drama people experience as they move through life—turning points, struggles, resolution, and new questions. Different excerpts from Scripture, art, and music about Mary are part of each person's journey with Mary.

Therefore, in each chapter, you will see a *person* in movement, on a journey, engaging with Scripture, art, music, and tradition. Stories capture the inner drama of people moving through stages of the spiritual life. Stories retain complexity without reducing human experience to bland, simplistic statements. Each person's story in this book retains its particularities, but each experience emanates from universal human desires we can all relate to.

These stories help us connect our personal spiritual journey to Mary without prescriptive instruction. My goal is not to tell you how to pray to Mary, but to leave you with questions, insights, and aids for your own spiritual journey.

Just as Mary is a living person in these stories, I too, am a living presence in these stories, being changed by what I hear, and recalling events of my life that resonate with the stories. I speak about my personal failings and painful life events, struggles to forgive myself and others, and smuggling rosaries to Cuban political and religious dissidents from the Communist regime.

I aim to present Mary as she has appeared to people in this book: not as a distant figure but as someone who called each of them to an intimate relationship with her and strengthened their bonds with the church. My hope is that this book will serve as a bridge, helping Catholics, Orthodox, and Protestants alike to rediscover Mary as she appears in salvation history and how she has been remembered through millennia of artistic and musical creations. By encountering Mary as a living presence among us, we can enrich our understanding of faith, deepen our spiritual lives, and perhaps even take steps toward greater unity in the body of Christ.

Through these seven different encounters with Mary—including one of my own—I aim to introduce people to various ways that Mary binds us to a living body of people of faith. She binds us to the beauty of the liturgy when we come together to worship God. She binds us to family, while, at the same time, she weaves our personal narratives into a story that transcends our immediate surroundings and helps us relate to others different from us. She's like the seed that sows the good soil. She leads us to the church. She brings unity out of division. She helps us overcome fear and find courage. In our personal confusion and cultural darkness, Mary models what it means to have new life in Christ. She's a mirror, always reflecting the light of her son Jesus into the world.

Meeting Mary in These Pages

In the forthcoming chapters, you will encounter a diverse group of people whose lives have been transformed through encounters with Mary. They are now Protestant, Catholic, and Orthodox, but three of them were seekers who were either raised in non-religious households or left the faith for decades before returning. I have known some of the people, like Evan, for more than a decade. Others, like Sally and Tammy, sought me out to share their stories about Mary after I began writing about Marian devotion and theology. Still others, like Aidan and James, have had distinguished careers in the arts and been collaborators with me in my work on theology and the arts. Al was my mentor and co-teacher. Below is a brief taste of what you can expect to encounter throughout these pages:

Chapter 1: Marks of Faith: Unveiling Mary's Presence in Cuba

The book opens with a trip to my mother's homeland of Cuba in 2005. Sweating at the airport in Havana while my bags were searched, I called out to Mary to protect me. Unexpectedly, I was released from the search, set free to carry out my mission of smuggling money, religious books, and rosaries to Cuban political and religious dissidents. On this and prior trips to Cuba with my mother, I found that although the faith had been outlawed for decades, Mary was alive in people's hearts, knitting together past, present, and future.

Chapter 2: A "Wild Marian Experience": Evan and the Irish Healing Well

Evan, whose story opened this chapter, was hesitant to reveal to his family or close friends his experiences with Mary. When he reached out to me to share this experience, we discussed how we both struggled with a "rationalistic worldview" that is skeptical about miracles. Although he was cautious about allowing one extraordinary experience to overtake his conviction that the life of prayer is mostly ordinary, he has been growing slowly more open to praying for Mary's intercession. When fearful of death during a dangerous hike on the Knife's Edge on Mount Katahdin in Maine, he instinctively called out to Mary for protection, repeating "Holy Mary, Mother of God, pray for us NOW!" His love for Mary as his spiritual mother has edified his relationship with Christ and helped him maintain his church involvement even when human personalities enter into conflict.

Chapter 3: A Compassionate Witness: Al Raboteau and Mary at the Cross

After the publication of his 1978 book *Slave Religion: The "Invisible Institution" in the Antebellum South*, which explores slaves' conversions to Christianity and the controversial theme of redemptive suffering, Albert J. Raboteau rose to academic fame but drifted from the Catholic faith of his childhood and fell into a deep personal crisis. One day, at an exhibition of Russian icons, Al felt Mary's compassionate gaze penetrating his heart. He began a slow return to faith, participating in an Eastern Orthodox Church with its embodied rituals, chants, and love for the Mother of God. He grew to see how much of the African American church experience he had written about echoed Marian themes, including forgiveness and compassion. After years of friendship and collaboration between us, I visited Al in 2021 as he was nearing death. The final words he spoke to me at barely a whisper, "Pray for the suffering," reinforced Mary's example at the foot of the cross: standing witness to unjust suffering without abandoning hope and offering her compassion.

Chapter 4: A Tear in the World: Sally's Life-Saving Encounter with Mary

After reading an article I wrote about a pilgrimage to Fátima, Sally reached out to me with a surprising revelation: "Mary saved my life." Sally was raised without religious faith but joined a United Methodist Church as a young adult. Early into her marriage, when she experienced three successive miscarriages, she had extraordinary visions of Mary. She recounted to me how Mary appeared to her through what she called "a tear in the world." She saw a woman with dark hair in blue floating above an ocean at night, which reminded me of the woman described in Revelation 12:1, as an allegorical representation of Mary. But Sally had no knowledge of Mary in Scripture when the visions started. As the visions continued, Mary led Sally to seek what turned out to be a life-saving medical visit for her, but not the baby she carried in her body. Despite Sally's unspeakable pain and suffering, Mary's maternal presence helped her hold on to her faith, see in Scripture the many ways that Jesus promises to be with us in our suffering, and discern God's mysterious workings in her life.

Chapter 5: Signs of Human Dignity: Aidan Hart and Sacred Art

During a lecture delivered at Princeton Theological Seminary in 2023, master iconographer Aidan Hart asked the audience: "Do I view other people as my competitors? As my enemies? . . . Or do I see all others as living icons of God, potential saints, amazing and unique beings, small gods, sons and daughters of the Most High?" Aidan shared his remarkable conversion to Christianity through reading the Bible on his own as a young seeker, and then through close mentorship in a Baptist church. His desire to unite his biblical faith with his vocation to make art led him to study Orthodox teachings on art. He joined the Orthodox church and lived as a monk for twelve years before returning to lay life. His sacred art adorns Catholic, Orthodox, and Protestant churches in twenty-five countries. The anointing screen he designed for King Charles III's 2024 coronation, just one of several commissions from the king, was seen by millions. Through his writing, lectures, and art, Aidan is passionate to evangelize culture by reminding everyone of their dignity as children of God.

Chapter 6: Echoes of the Annunciation: James MacMillan and Mary's Creative Inspiration

"Perhaps it is not too fanciful to say that every musical composition is a little incarnation," Sir James MacMillan told me when I asked him about the inspiration behind his musical compositions. As a young man growing up in a poor family in a depressed area of Scotland, James struggled to unite his Catholic faith with his desire to compose music. For decades, as he rose to be one of the most highly regarded composers in the world, he largely never discussed his faith with secular friends. One day, he shared with a journalist his belief that his work is divinely inspired. Her astonished, yet open, reaction to that statement, which she called "*avant-garde*," led him to further ponder how Scripture and tradition can help us see composers as being called to be vessels of God, analogous to Mary being the vessel through which Christ entered the world. In James's life and music, Mary is not just an object, but a leader who shows him how to draw in ever more complex musical elements and compose something beautiful. He describes human co-creation with God as echoes of the annunciation.

Chapter 7: "Am I Worthy?": Tammy Peterson Follows Mary to Jesus and the Church

"Mary called me to Christ, and Christ called me to the church." Facing terminal cancer with ten months to live, Tammy Peterson, the wife of public speaker and author Jordan

Peterson, experienced a moment of overwhelming grace and worthiness when she shared the news with her son. The pain in his eyes reflected her motherly love back on her, and the Holy Spirit entered her body. When in the hospital fighting for her life, Tammy remembered the Lord's Prayer, which she learned as a child before she rejected Christianity as a teenager and resolving never to set foot in church again. A Catholic friend visited her daily in the hospital and taught her to pray the rosary, a traditional Catholic devotion of meditating on Scripture while reciting the Lord's Prayer and the Hail Mary prayer. After her recovery, Tammy committed to a daily Christian prayer life at home. She searched the Scriptures, received mentorship from a priest, and five years after her near-death experience, she became a Roman Catholic. Mary's full cooperation with God reminds Tammy to surrender her ego; Mary's spiritual motherhood helps Tammy seek to do only God's will every day.

Conclusion: "Am I Not Your Mother?"

In this closing chapter, I reflect on how my spiritual struggles have slowly loosened the grip of rationalism and self-will. In 2001, I faced a grave temptation while attending a Vodou ceremony in Haiti. For a moment, I opened my heart to the spirits moving around me, but then I quickly took refuge under Mary's mantle. Shortly thereafter, I learned that my father was near death and begged Mary to help me. Time and again, I need to return to Mary's protective embrace in the battle against evil spirits not only outside but inside me. While at Mass celebrating Our Lady of Guadalupe not long ago, I once again allowed myself to embrace spiritual childhood and ponder Mary's mystical presence in and around me. She spoke to my heart the same words she had spoken audibly to St. Juan Diego centuries before: "Am I not your mother?"

Annotated Bibliography

This annotated bibliography presents readers with resources that will help them continue their exploration of Mary across the rich landscape of Christian traditions, both past and present. The resources I briefly summarize explore Mary's presence in both the Old and New Testaments, the history of Christianity, personal devotions to Mary, and liturgical feasts that commemorate Mary.

An Invitation to the Journey

Mary's presence has shaped Christian faith and culture for two millennia. Mary is present in the Scriptures; she is present in the writings of the church fathers; she is present in central doctrines of Christianity, like the incarnation. Mary is present in the great cathedrals and works of art dedicated to her and in the devotional practices of countless believers throughout history. She is present with her son Jesus, with whom she shared the most powerful bond possible: that of mother and son.

As I shared with Evan, when you begin to discern Mary's presence in your faith, you just might realize she's been there all along, accompanying you on the whole journey. We can forget our mother, but she can't forget us.

The strength of Mary's example resides not in grand gestures but in her patient presence, and in small acts of faith and love that keep the divine flame alive when all seems dark.

I hope this book encourages greater receptivity and openness to a relationship with Mary as a spiritual mother—a living, active, tender presence binding us to the Trinity and the church.

By getting to know Mary as your spiritual mother, I hope you to get to know Christ more intimately as your savior, learn to perceive the Holy Spirit inspiring your life, and experience more deeply the love of God the Father.

Chapter 1

Marks of Faith

Unveiling Mary's Presence in Cuba

Exile and Return

The night before my 2005 flight to Cuba, I stood in my living room with Francisco, who helped me pack my bags to avoid detection at customs.[1]

"Would you please light a candle for my mother at the Shrine of Our Lady of Charity?"

Francisco, an Afro-Cuban from Santiago, had immigrated to America two years prior. Though fear of the Communist regime had kept his mother from taking him to church while in Cuba, she had secretly baptized him twenty-eight years earlier as a baby.

Francisco's eyes brimmed with tears as he handed me a letter to take to his mother's grave in Cuba. I gazed back into Francisco's eyes for several seconds, trying to be present to his pain, just as my mother had been present to the people we met when we traveled together to Cuba a few years earlier. I silently prayed that Mary would wrap Francisco in her mantle. I also prayed for protection as we wrapped about fifty rosaries in my clothes, hoping to avoid detection at the border. This was my seventh trip to Cuba since 1994—and my riskiest one yet. Each time I traveled to Cuba, I brought more items the regime deemed subversive, such as music by Cuban artists whose only crime was leaving the country and never returning.

I stuffed $4,000 cash in $20 bills into my handbag. An influential Cuban-American leader had given me the cash, as there were no ATMs from which I could withdraw US dollars in Cuba. On a small piece of paper tucked inside my clothes, I had scribbled the names and amounts of money to give to religious and political dissidents who fought against the regime, facing harassment and imprisonment. I placed a miniature soccer ball for the son of an imprisoned dissident and a DVD player for a Catholic priest in Santiago de Cuba in my suitcase.

To conceal my true intentions, I flew to Mexico to join tourists heading to Cuba. From Cancún, I boarded an Aeroméxico flight to Havana, donning a large, wide sombrero and bright pink lipstick, a caricature of a tourist in search of sunshine and salsa dancing. On the immigration form, I listed "Hotel Nacional" as my accommodations, a national landmark showcased in *The Godfather Part II* as the site of a meeting of mafia leaders. Revealing the truth—that I was staying with relatives in Havana—would expose that I was wearing a costume and hoping to evade detection as the member of a Cuban family who fought the Communist takeover of Cuba.

At the Havana airport, a customs agent sifted through my bags, her Spanish slow and deliberate as if she were speaking to a child. I shrugged, feigning ignorance, and boldly lied, speaking in English: "I don't speak Spanish."

I restrained my instinct to respond, nod, gasp, or let my eyes reveal that I understood her questions, fearing my body would betray that I comprehended every word.

It was the X-ray machine that betrayed me. The customs agent pulled the DVD player from my bag, her eyes glaring at mine. My heart sank. Although I had carefully removed all the packaging from the new items I brought, I had forgotten to remove the small plastic cover over the screen of the DVD player.

"It's mine," I lied once more, speaking English and pointing to my chest for emphasis. "Mine. It's mine."

The agent pointed to another line and escorted me there for a more thorough search. Ahead of me, a German tourist stood helplessly as two agents dismantled his suitcase, unrolled his socks and underwear, and analyzed his face for the slightest twitch of anxiety while they unzipped the vinyl covering inside his suitcase.

My imagination roamed through various possibilities of what might happen to me next. Frantically, I tried to think of even more lies I could tell that would help me escape.

Sweat dripped down my spine in the sweltering heat of the non-air-conditioned airport. How would I explain the letters I was carrying to Francisco's family? Would they discover the $4,000 in cash? What if they found the names of the dissidents written on a piece of paper hidden inside my clothes?

I worried that if my charade was busted and they discovered my identity as a Cuban American aligned with the regime's adversaries inside Cuba and in the US, I would join the ranks of those who were harassed, interrogated, and deported. I feared that I would crumble under pressure, break down in tears, and, in exchange for being sent home instead of to jail, betray the names, locations, and activities of dissidents.

Outwardly, I appeared stoic. The heavy, tropical air filled my lungs while silent prayers ascended from within me, gathering force like the white foam that blossoms atop waves before they break against the wall protecting Havana's sunbaked promenade, known as the Malecón. The silent litany of prayers flowed out, pleading for protection. "*Santa María, siempre virgen; Jesús Cristo; San Ignacio de Loyola, sácame de aquí!*" (Blessed Mary, forever virgin; Jesus Christ; Saint Ignatius of Loyola, get me out of here!)

Although I was physically alone during this confrontation, I suddenly felt spiritually accompanied by Christ and his devoted followers, including the brave dissidents, missionaries, and laypeople in Cuba who refused to be intimidated by the atheist regime.

The first agent who searched my bags discovered the DVD player. He glared at me and whispered in Spanish to his colleague, "Frequent tourists are more likely to carry prohibited items. Let's find out how often she visits Cuba." Then, booming in Spanish, a tall Afro-Cuban man asked me, "When was the last time you visited Cuba?"

In response, I held up my hands, fingers spread apart, and shouted in English, "TWO ZERO ZERO TWO." My reply came too quickly; I worried I had blown my cover. "Go over there!" I was commanded in Spanish. Panic coursed through my veins as I scanned the room for another search area. "No, no, over there. There!" the customs guard repeated, directing me and my bags toward the airport exit—no further questions asked.

Outside the airport exit, my cousin Claudia called my name and rushed to embrace me. But I pushed her away, whispering, "*Vamos, rápido!*" (Let's go, fast). As we drove to her apartment in central Havana, I recounted my narrow escape. Claudia appeared unfazed and reminded me that for Cubans, harassment is commonplace.

I didn't dare tell Claudia about all the contraband I was carrying—lying to her was essential to protecting her, lest the local members of the Committee for the Defense of the Revolution discover that she was harboring a relative from the US and come around asking questions.

I clutched a rosary that night, praying countless Hail Marys as I tried to sleep. What if during this risky trip I was exposed as a *gusana*, (which translates literally to "worm" and is used as slang to refer to a so-called traitor)? Would I break down sobbing under interrogation, and trade information about dissidents in exchange for leaving on the next flight to Miami? My body rocked back and forth as my mind struggled to hold on to courage. My hands rubbed my rosary beads with no immediate effect on my psyche. The task before me—to spend two weeks endlessly code-switching and costume-changing to be either an American tourist or a local Cuban—seemed impossible.

Finding Mary, Our Lady of Sorrows

As my anxiety kept me awake, my mind drifted back to when I traveled to Cuba with my mother in 1999. I was in my early twenties, nearly the same age my mother had been when she was imprisoned by the Communist regime in Cuba in 1961. Part of what had given her the confidence to return to Cuba decades after she fled was the 1998 visit of Pope John Paul

II to the island. I remember being glued to the television as the vehemently anti-Communist Catholic pope from behind the Iron Curtain visited a nation that had expelled nearly all priests and religious sisters, closed all churches and religious schools, and made atheism a central principle of the Cuban Constitution.

One of Pope John Paul II's stops was at the Shrine of Our Lady of Charity near the eastern city of Santiago de Cuba. The shrine commemorates Mary's appearance to three men, two indigenous and one enslaved, who nearly perished at sea in 1600. The three men prayed for protection from Mary and saw a vision of her. When they reached shore, a piece of wood bore Mary's image, inscribed with the words, "I am the Virgin of Charity."

A shrine was built for her at El Cobre, a copper mine on the island's eastern end, and it has been expanded over time. Because El Cobre was the site where slaves in Cuba were granted freedom in 1801, Nuestra Señora de la Caridad del Cobre (Our Lady of Charity of the Copper Mine) became a symbol of freedom for the Cuban nation, especially during the Cuban fight for independence from Spain at the turn of the twentieth century.

Pope John Paul II's 1998 visit resulted in slight loosening of the restrictions Cuba had placed on religious worship. Cuban exiles like my mother, who had previously been unable to return, were now allowed to visit. The prospect of going back to Cuba brought horrible memories to my mother: she recalled being locked in a women's prison and hearing of executions. Although her father's life was spared and he fled to the United States, several of her college classmates were shot by a firing squad. Her uncle was condemned to death for plotting to overthrow the Communist government but died of natural causes in a Cuban prison before his sentence was executed.

As I had seen so many people in war-torn Central America rebuild bridges—literally and symbolically—I longed for the Cuban people to reunite. After graduating from Yale University in 1995, I worked for three years at the Arias Foundation for Peace and Human Development, based in Costa Rica. I visited communities that had been established on former battlefields in Nicaragua, El Salvador, and Guatemala. Millions of lives were lost in the brutal civil wars in those countries. From the ashes of such devastation, seeds of reconciliation were planted, and land was being re-harvested.

Could it now be possible to rebuild bridges with the people of Cuba? After landing in Havana, my mother and I drove through the beautiful countryside, searching for the village where her family had operated a sugar mill.

"There it is!" my mother exclaimed, pointing at a giant tower. "El Ingenio Dolores." We drove along a road lined with palm trees and parked our Russian Lada near the *batey*, the village surrounding the Sugar Mill named for Our Lady of Sorrows, near the town of Pedro Betancourt in the province of Matanzas, about an hour's drive from Havana.

As we stepped out into the humid Cuban air during that summer of 1999, my mother took a deep breath, savoring the scent of sugar being refined at the mill. The natural beauty was breathtaking—towering palm trees and the vibrant red leaves of a *flamboyan* tree welcomed us. The village remained practically unchanged. The only indicators of the passage of time were the dilapidation and abandonment of the same buildings that had stood there forty years earlier, including mostly small homes, an abandoned gas station, and the boarded-up church.

We were welcomed at the *batey* next to the sugar mill by villagers, one of whom brought us the baptismal cards of my family members who had been baptized in the local church that my family had built. With a warm smile, she said, "I thought maybe you would return someday, and you might want to see these!"

Stained-Glass Windows

Our hosts at El Dolores guided us to the former village church, which had been converted into a movie theater after the Cuban Revolution. Now the building stood vacant, its windows mere shells covered with wooden panels. Inside, grass grew wildly on the dirt floor. The few rays of light that streamed in flickered like a candle in a dark room at night.

We were taken to a villager's house, one of the lay Catholics who had not abandoned his faith despite the persecution. Like many Cuban homes, his backyard was filled with various knickknacks and random pieces of equipment. In a country where the economy had come to a standstill after the Soviet collapse, every object had countless potential uses. He smiled as he led us to something special, removing one wooden beam after another to uncover a large black tarp.

"*Las vitrinas*!" my mother exclaimed as the tarp was pulled back, seeing two stained glass windows which the villages had saved when the church was closed, and all its religious artifacts destroyed. We admired a stained-glass window framed by roses. In one window, Mary held Jesus on her lap, surrounded by angels and shepherds who were worshiping him. As Mary is often pictured in a garden to symbolize how she has helped to reopen the doors of paradise, the window had a border of roses. The roses my mother had searched for were gone from the overgrown garden in front of her grandparents' house in the village. Still, I thought perhaps, just perhaps, this image signified that Mary's motherhood was the soil that allowed roses to bloom in people's hearts even amidst religious and political persecution.

The second stained-glass window spared from the iconoclasm of the Cuban Communist Revolution depicted Mary standing at the foot of the cross, her hands crossed, her eyes distressed, her heart wrenched with grief. From the cross, Jesus had cried out in anguish: "My God, my God why hast thou forsaken me?" (Matthew 27:46) How many Cubans, feeling forsaken after all these years of separation from loved ones, had asked God the same question?

Cubans at El Dolores had few opportunities for Mass, confession, or sacraments for decades. Yet the slogans of the revolution, such as "socialism or death," "down with the Yanquis," (the Spanish spelling of Yankees, used as slang to refer to all Americans) had not erased the memory of fundamental Christian prayers. Groups met secretly to pray the rosary, reciting the Our Father and Hail Marys. In a land where the Bible was viewed as a tool for government subversion, the rosary, which consists of a series of meditations on twenty scenes from Scripture, served to preserve the memory of the faith.

The Cuban *patria*—fatherland—had placed the so-called universal march of socialism above all other goals, dismantling images that might obstruct the atheism deemed necessary to supposedly claim one's place in history and create a utopian society where pain and suffering cease to exist. Yet, the people at El Dolores, along with many others I encountered in Cuba, remembered their mother who cradled her son in her arms as a baby, then watched him suffer on the cross, a victim of persecution.

Mary's steadfast presence at the foot of the cross shown in one of the stained-glass windows reminded people that Mary had lived through tumultuous violence. She was a mother who understood the Cuban Christians' longings, fears, and desires to keep hope alive. The fire of faith was hidden in Cuba, but it undeniably radiated warmth in the human connections we forged while there.

My mother imitated Mary's hope at the foot of the cross. She expressed profound joy at reconnecting with her past even amidst devastating sorrow. She listened patiently for hours to others' painful stories of illness, betrayal, and loneliness.

One woman told my mother how, in desperation over her daughter's illness, she had prayed to Mary, but her daughter was not healed. Out of despair, she tore a picture of Our Lady of Charity from a calendar on her wall and stomped on it. Not long after, her daughter was healed. Just as God intervened despite that mother's anger, my mother did not demand perfect faith or an apology before offering her compassion. My mother recognized how the woman's acknowledgment of her moment of hopelessness could bring her to a deeper faith.

"Our Lady of Charity understands a mother's desperation

when her child is suffering,"[2] my mother recorded in her memoir, *Leaving Cuba: One Family's Journey to Freedom.* Although I was tempted to critique this woman's actions as blasphemous, I also recognized my hypocrisy. How often had I lashed out in anger at God for not answering my prayers over rather trivial matters, only to have them answered later?

The power of maternal compassion to serve as a balm for painful memories and to nurture hope became even more apparent when my mother visited a man whose son had died by suicide. In his living room, his wife lay catatonic while he recounted how his son had set himself on fire. The room's only decoration was a 1950s British motorcycle draped with two pictures of Our Lady of Charity. My mother, like Mary, looked at this hopeless situation and perceived that this father was clinging to at least some belief in God. This family, engulfed by darkness, clung to the images of Our Lady of Charity as drowning souls might reach for a lifeline—a desperate appeal to something transcendent. My mother listened to his stories, connecting personally to this grieving father, hoping that their painfully honest conversation might lead to him allow God back into his life.

In another village where my mother had lived, we attended Mass at a church where the walls remained, though the roof had collapsed. A woman entered with flowers as an offering for Our Lady of Charity. She had never set foot in a church before, yet she entered this roofless building to experience Mass for the first time. She shared that she spent most of her time alone at home; however, by bringing flowers to an image of Mary, she made a tangible connection to an immaterial reality she sensed was real.

As my mother sat listening to stories of isolation, hardship, and desperation, she did not try to fix every situation or judge anyone's reactions—even angry ones. I began to understand why the image and memory of Our Lady of Charity, her real presence, persisted in the privacy of so many Cuban homes. Like my mother in so many forlorn living rooms, Mary offered not ready-made solutions that sound like clichés, but a warm, motherly embrace.

In public places, the salty air and high winds regularly eroded the triumphant faces of the then-still-living Fidel Castro and the long-dead *guerrilla* hero Che Guevara painted on walls and billboards across Cuba. However, in private homes, I saw no images of Communist heroes. No one spoke of Fidel or Che as if they were friends. Instead, Mary—nearly always depicted as Cuba's patroness and protectress, Our Lady of Charity—reigned inside Cuban homes. Time and again, people referred to Mary not as a figure from distant history but as someone close to them in their struggles. In his speeches, Fidel often spoke of the Cuban people's history as beginning with the triumph of the Cuban Revolution, effectively erasing the past prior to Cuban Communism. But in people's homes, Mary's love flowed as if from a deep well moving from the distant past into the present, watering the Cuban soil with hope for a future that united rather than divided Cuban families.

Inspired by the courage and faith of the people I encountered during my trips to Cuba with my mother, I returned several more times without her by my side, each visit involving greater risks to support religious leaders and political dissidents.

From Havana to Santiago

Having made it through customs without being searched during my trip in 2005, I prepared for the challenging task of distributing the gifts I had brought—including clothes, medicine, and surgical mesh for Marcos, a doctor and friend from my previous trips to Cuba, who was an adult convert to Catholicism. After a few days with my cousin Claudia in Havana, I boarded a bus for Santiago, where elderly religious sisters accepted the rosaries with tearful gratitude, telling me how much I resembled my mother, with whom they had studied at a girls' school in Havana run by the religious sisters of the Society of the Sacred Heart. Francisco's family gratefully received the shoes, the forbidden music, and the letters. With a small group of Cuban lay missionaries, I visited the Sanctuary of Our Lady of Charity and, as promised, lit a candle for Francisco's mother.

One day, I visited Santiago's Catholic Cathedral, called Our Lady of the Assumption. A priest escorted me into a private room where the wife of an imprisoned dissident awaited. She beamed when I gave her a soccer ball for her son. Then, I handed her $300, a small fortune in Cuba. She was one of the Damas en Blanco (Ladies in White), who gathered to advocate for the release of their husbands imprisoned during one of the many crackdowns on democratic movements in Cuba. I admired women like her who refused to abandon their loved ones, who had been publicly humiliated, falsely accused, and brutally punished. Their white clothing symbolized peace, and their public gatherings served as a sign of defiance.

A flicker of hope danced in her eyes as she asked if I

might know someone who could help broker a deal to release her husband from prison. I jotted down notes in my journal, promising her I would deliver the message to influential Cuban Americans I knew were eager to assist her.

Danger at the *Paladar*

The memories of my mother's calm compassion faded as I faced yet another moment of danger during my 2005 trip. One of the people I was asked to visit, a dissident and independent journalist named José, asked to me to a *paladar* (a mini-restaurant for tourists in a Cuban home), run by his sister. When I arrived and was escorted to a back room, José pointed to the window where a policeman stood watching.

"My sister made a mistake. She called me and said a tourist wanted to talk to me. My phone is tapped," he explained. "The police followed me here. Next, they will follow you."

My hands shook as I replaced the memory disc filled with photos of dissidents' wives with tourist snapshots, concealing the disc with the essential pictures inside my clothes.

"Listen," José said, noticing the fear in my eyes, "nothing in the Cuban Constitution prohibits Cubans from speaking to foreigners. Even if they stop and question you, they can't do anything. The police only want to intimidate you."

José asked me to sit on the balcony and slowly savor a beer to maintain my tourist charade. Twenty minutes later, I found myself once again in the back room with José, my notebook open and my pen ready to document the human rights violations he urgently wanted the world to acknowledge. Names, dates, and instances of harassment poured out, a long list of abuses committed by a government intent on silencing its critics at any cost. José implored me to share with human rights organizations all the specific incidents he knew of the regime's extensive network of spies and secret police trampling on Cubans' fundamental rights to free expression, movement, and dissent.

Compared to the courage José displayed, the $200 I gave him felt like a small gesture of support. When I left the *paladar*, I could sense the officer's gaze following me. I knew I could not lead him to my hosts' home lest I implicate them. Instead, my feet took me to the cathedral.

When I arrived at the plaza and turned to ascend the cathedral stairs, I glanced back, my eyes meeting the policeman's gaze.

"Your power means nothing in God's house. I *dare* you to follow me into this church," I said silently and defiantly. In a country where no one speaks the truth and everyone wears a mask, even if I did not speak audibly, my intense stare served as an act of resistance against his intimidation.

Despite the outward display of defiance, my heart pounded with fear just as surely as my feet pounded up the stairs of the cathedral. I approached the front pew and knelt before the altar, pleading for protection. The words I had heard from Paul's second letter to the Corinthians (4:8–9) during Mass just a few days earlier at the cathedral echoed in my mind: "We are afflicted in every way, but not crushed; perplexed, but not driven to despair; persecuted, but not forsaken; struck down, but not destroyed."

I stared up at the cross. Part of me wanted the policeman to enter the cathedral, confident he could not suppress his sense that God rules over everything. And he sees right into our hearts. The other part of me hoped my wish would not come true. Maybe I wasn't as courageous as I believed I was and my weakness would be exposed.

I remained almost entirely still for twenty minutes, praying the rosary on my knees. With each bead, I lifted in prayer the names of the people I had met in Cuba. It felt as though all the eyes of the saints and Our Lady of Charity were upon me, sustaining me. I was visiting the persecuted, but I was not alone. My mask was ripped off, but I prayed for help not to give in. The church dedicated to Mary served as my sanctuary during those uncertain twenty minutes.

When I exited the cathedral, the policeman was nowhere to be seen. I breathed a sigh of relief that my bravado had not been put to the test.

Marked as a Traitor

"*Margarita, tú estás marcada*," my hostess warned when I finally returned from the cathedral in 2005. You are marked.

Throughout the week, my prolonged and enigmatic absences indicated to her that I was visiting dissidents. Her language was coded, but I knew what she meant when she said I was marked.

Perhaps I escaped a few times during this trip, but with that one sentence she warned me that it was only a matter of time before I would be caught. I remained silent. I could not deny that what she had accurately assumed explained my long absences—that I was visiting dissidents. Nor did I reveal my fear that she was right. The risks were becoming too high for me. Torn between wanting to help dissidents and the fear of being caught, I wondered if this might be my last trip to Cuba.

A few days later, my friend Marcos drove me to the airport in Santiago to fly home. My jaw clenched as I waved my hands and raged against the abuses I had heard about.

Cuban Americans frequently wonder why those on the island don't fight the regime more, a concern I repeated.

"This place is a huge prison!" I yelled. "Why don't people fight harder?"

"Margarita," Marcos said gently, "you are about to board a plane. One hour later, you will be in Miami, taking a hot shower and enjoying a *café con leche* (coffee and hot milk). If I could join you on that plane, I would. But I'm not allowed to leave Cuba."

His response changed my train of thought. I was, in fact, moved deeply by the endurance and courage of those who were harassed and whose loved ones were jailed. I admired people like Marcos, who performed daily acts of love and service, not demanding that God instantly relieve all their burdens or fill their bellies with treats to compensate for their suffering, as I often do.

"Somehow, in this atheist country, God granted me the gift of faith," Marcos continued. "I'm grateful to have found a community of love in the Catholic Church. After I drop you off, I'm going to visit an elderly woman who lives alone. I'll bring her some milk and spend time talking with her. You may not think I'm doing much, but God gave me the gift of faith, and I will keep helping the lonely and abandoned people around me."

His fraternal rebuke stirred my conscience. I had overlooked that resistance to evil doesn't always require grand gestures. Marcos reminded me that the steady presence that refuses to allow fear or hatred to prevail holds a power greater than any government. Refusing to wallow in self-pity and instead sharing the love of God with a lonely person is a powerful act of resistance.

As my plane lifted off from Cuban soil, I carried many marks—not just the government's label of *gusana* but also the deep imprint of lessons learned from Cuba's many heroes. Their acts of courage, charity, and mercy showed me that the kingdom of heaven belongs not to those who rule indiscriminately over others, but to those who, like Mary, remain steadfast in the darkness, trusting in a light that no earthly power can extinguish.

Gazing out the window at the turquoise waters of the Caribbean Sea that divides the two sides of the Cuban family, I wondered if I would ever return to Cuba. Once in Miami, I met with those who had entrusted me with specific tasks during my trips to Cuba, delivering information about abuses and letters of gratitude for the money and goods sent.

Inside my heart, I continued to grapple with what Marcos helped me to see about myself: I am too focused on controlling outcomes, which often obscures the need to simply be present to others in love, regardless of our power to take away their pain.

My travels to Cuba—first with my mother, then alone—taught me that Mary's protection isn't about shielding us from all danger or suffering. Mary accompanies us through the valley of tears, helping us maintain our faith when everything around us seems designed to destroy it. In visiting my mother's homeland, I had grown closer to my mother in heaven, leading me to her son. I became more aware of the many times that, like the Cubans I met, I turned to Mary as a refuge, pleading with her as my spiritual mother to give me fortitude and bind the wounds of the people I met. Although I have not returned to Cuba since 2005, each bead on every rosary I left behind in Cuba marked an Our Father or a Hail Mary. Every prayer coming out of the Cuban people's lips showed me that no earthly power could erase the deep mark of faith in the memory of the Cuban people.

The Church Reopened

In the years following our first visit to El Dolores, our family had raised enough money in the United States to reopen the church. The beautiful stained-glass windows were put back in place. Now, sunlight could dance radiantly through the stained-glass window of Mary with a border of roses, shining light on parched souls who had faithfully waited for their house of worship to reopen. Villagers had also hidden the *sagrario*, the tabernacle, where the Host, the consecrated Eucharist, is reserved inside a Catholic Church. This village sanctuary was open again. The waters of faith flowed into those who walked into a church for the first time, seeking grace and healing. On their journey home to God, they were embraced by a mother who led them toward the paradise lost, opening up a pathway to God that had been restored through her son's suffering, death and resurrection.

Christ was once again the center of the village; he now had

a home again in El Dolores, waiting for his separated brethren to seek him as my mother had come seeking to reconnect to her past. Mary, his mother, is present in those windows, surrounded by roses, holding the infant Jesus and standing next to him at his cross. She remains there, inviting people home to God their Father, not promising freedom from the cross but teaching us how to find the roses among thorns. Mary's exceptional cooperation with grace, and her steadfast presence at the cross, symbolize how beauty and hope can flourish in unexpected places.

A few years after the church was rebuilt, the Cuban government dismantled the sugar mill in El Dolores. Piece by piece, the giant machinery that had sustained hundreds, if not thousands, of lives was gone.

But as my mother noted in her memoir, even as the sugar mill was gone, "God's house was standing restored. It stood there with the people after the sugar mill was gone, reminding everyone that God is with us, always in our need, and remains with us no matter what darkness."[3]

My trips to Cuba showed me how Mary helps us to face painful memories with hope in God's promise that he will never abandon his children. During his 1998 visit, Pope John Paul II prayed at the Shrine of Our Lady of Charity and spoke about how only a hope grounded in faith would allow Cubans to unite what politics has torn apart. Pope John Paul II spoke to the Cuban people about how Mary would "gather together your peoples scattered throughout the world."[4] The Cuban nation can only become "a home of brothers and sisters" through reconciliation that grows from self-giving love. The title for Mary, Our Lady of Charity, he said, "evokes thoughts of the God who is Love" and "recalls the new commandment given by Jesus," that is, to love one another as he has loved us. Pope John Paul II understood what I witnessed: Mary's "name and image are sculpted in the mind and heart of every Cuban, both within and outside the country, as a sign of hope and a focus of fraternal communion." Mary came "to visit our people and wished to remain with us as Mother and Lady of Cuba, throughout its pilgrimage along the paths of history."

During my trips, I saw how God's love had not been extinguished in Cuba. Mary was present in Cuban homes, such as in the villager who hid stained-glass windows wrapped in a tarp and protected by wooden beams and guarded by his steadfastness in the faith. The secret rosaries prayed during decades of atheist rule by Catholics who refused to renounce their faith and the offering of a woman new to the faith who brought flowers to Mary's image at a roofless church were all expressions of Mary's motherhood of the faithful across the millennia.

Reflecting on those journeys now, my branding as a *gusana* is nothing compared to the deeper mark of my belonging into a community of faith that transcends borders of nations and time. Mary's presence reminds us that simply to be present, to witness, to remember, and to pray for a unity among brothers and sisters are all acts of love that can touch human hearts in a way no totalitarian regime ever could.

Chapter 2

A "*Wild Marian Experience*"

Evan and the Irish Healing Well

Do Miracles Happen Today?

When I first met Evan in 2013, ten years before he texted me about his "wild Marian experience" that I touched on in the introduction, he was an undergraduate student from the rural South studying classics and engineering at an urban, secular college campus in the Northeast. His gentle southern accent and carefully chosen words conveyed a maturity beyond his years, even though his slight build and youthful face often led people to underestimate his age. During Evan's fall break of his sophomore year of college, he attended a seminar for students from all over the Northeast, where I was one of several professors discussing the relevance of great books of the classical liberal arts tradition.

At that seminar, we connected over a meal and shared about our families, our love of learning, and our Christian faith. Even after he graduated from college and moved away, over the years, Evan and I found time to meet up for pizza, ice cream, or coffee and stay updated on each other's faith and work.

During our first lengthy conversation about his surprising encounter with Mary, Evan searched for words to express the profound sense of intimacy with God and gratitude for Mary as a spiritual mother he had felt. He also yearned to connect that experience to his biblical faith. The few friends he shared it with—a Pentecostal man, a woman into New Age spirituality, and his sister, who is Evangelical—believed something profound had occurred during his encounter with Mary but knew little about Mary in the Bible. His sister remarked that it was fine to love Mary, provided he loved Scripture too. His New Age friend believed in the power of feminine godlike spirits, but Evan believed Mary was human, not a goddess. His Pentecostal friend encouraged him to be grateful for God's healing.

Evan shared his experience with me, hoping that as a Catholic woman, my knowledge of Mary in Scripture and theology might help him perceive more deeply how God was at work in his life. When I asked Evan to share his story in detail, he first turned to the harmony he felt between his inner life and the natural beauty of the surroundings. His love for hiking had taken him to several spots in Europe, where he marveled at how the Bible he revered was likewise revered by monks in places like the Skellig Islands in Ireland, near where he had his encounter with Mary. These monks had preserved the Gospels and other books during periods of invasions. The monastery on the Skellig Islands was founded in the sixth century and endured Viking attacks in 824 AD that decimated many other monasteries in present-day Ireland and Great Britain. Although many religious artifacts and manuscripts were destroyed by the Viking raids, the monks on Skellig Island were protected due to their remote location and challenging topography. With great care and skill, the monks copied the gospels and other religious texts, illuminating the manuscripts with art.

"Civilization was falling apart. And these monks sustained a life of learning and prayer that lit the fire of civilization anew much later," Evan said. The beautiful works of civilization—including monasteries of great learning—that Christians had built and maintained for two thousand years demonstrated to Evan countless concrete ways that faith and learning, including scientific advancement, flourished hand in hand.

Driving through the wind and fog, looking out at the islands and pondering history, had mysteriously led him to follow his instincts at the healing waters, recite a beautiful prayer to Mary that he found, and open his heart to God. When he did, he experienced an incredible feeling of spiritual consolation and physical healing flowing into him.

"I was tired from a lot of traveling, and I had a terrible throat ache. I had taken some medicine, but it just got worse," he explained. By kneeling, opening his heart, and following his instincts, he his body and his soul were transformed.

I wondered: "Would you call what happened in Ireland a miracle?"

Evan took a few seconds to collect his thoughts. Speaking slowly, he stated that he believed in miracles, "at least those in the Bible." But he was hesitant to frame his healing as a miracle, in part because he'd been infected by what he called "a Western, disenchanted worldview."

This phrase is often used to describe how science and reason have stripped the world of mystery and meaning. A disenchanted, rational worldview severs the natural from the supernatural, creating a chasm between a faith that focuses on mystery and grace and a faith that focuses on using our reason to learn the word of God and act in accordance with it. Some ways of practicing Christianity might emphasize ethical behavior rather than miracles or sacraments. But if the path to holiness nearly eradicates the idea of a living, moving supernatural presence in the world, then the result, far too often, is an approach to Christianity that is a kind of law-bound rationalism. Evan had too often encountered a dry intellectualism about Christian doctrine and morals with no language for an embodied experience of God's grace moving through us.

But Evan's experience at the well was a profoundly spiritual *and* embodied experience. Despite feeling changed both physically and spiritually, Evan hesitated to call the experience a miracle. Rather than analyze the experience too much, he sought to preserve his wonder at the event, emphasizing how God's grace had moved in mysterious ways during that moment. Many Christians Evan met in the Northeast, whether Catholic or Protestant, had embraced a hyper-intellectual approach to faith. "Too often when we talk about faith, we want to analyze every experience and measure it against one or another category. But this was so neat, it just doesn't seem right to put a label on it."

Evan believed that God had given him this exceptional experience for his "personal edification in the faith." He looked to Mary in Scripture to articulate a posture before a mysterious encounter. "My reaction is like Mary's reaction when Christ was born. What does the King James Bible say? She pondered these things, or she treasured these things in her heart," according to Luke 2:19. "I don't know how to interpret the experience except gratitude for our spiritual mother and the grace of God," he said, "but I am pondering and praying."

Evan knew that this exceptional experience was a special gift from God, and that gift reminded him that God's grace is at work more than we often realize. "God is very capable of revealing Himself to us in pedestrian ways. Our ordinary experiences are meaningful and legitimate expressions of God's grace." His exceptional experience in Ireland fortified his certainty of God's presence in ordinary life, even when he was not as keenly aware of it as he was at the healing well.

When I asked Evan if he was open to attending a weekday Catholic liturgy for an upcoming feast in honor of Mary, he readily agreed, curious to see how Catholics honored Mary through prayers recited and songs sung at Mass. Knowing how much he valued Scripture, I intentionally directed him to a parish led by priests of the Dominican order, whose charism includes a special focus on preaching.

I smiled when Evan texted, "Wow, did that priest open my eyes about the Scriptures! I never heard a Catholic talk so well about Scripture before." I had suggested that, after Mass, he could give thanks for his exceptional encounter with Mary by saying a prayer in front of a statue of her. Before attending the Mass, I had texted him the angel's words to Mary in Luke 1: 28: "Hail [Mary], full of grace, the Lord is with you!" And then, I added, that if he was comfortable, he could conclude with a petition at the end of the Hail Mary prayer that Catholics pray, "Holy Mary, Mother of God, pray for us sinners, now and at the hour of our death."

Evan recited the entire Hail Mary prayer in front of the statue. Nothing exceptional happened, but he did not expect it to. But that did not mean he discounted the power of those prayers. Rather, he spoke about how "the comfort of prayer, including prayer to Mary, isn't limited to exceptional experiences." Regular prayers with no seeming effect nonetheless edify us, he insisted. Expanding his understanding of how Christians pray, including the kneeling and bowing at Catholic Mass and saying prayers in front of statues, did not seem to him to violate anything in Scripture—his ultimate authority—or constitute idol worship.

Evan shared that at his local non-denominational church in the Northeast, they rented space from a Lutheran church with ornate stained-glass windows. He pointed out that "it's not too much mental gymnastics to realize praying to those statues of Mary is like looking at a stained-glass window." In fact, "the stained-glass window makes the light more intense or shows certain wavelengths. Just like having glasses helps me see the world around me, stained glass and statues help me see God in the world." He acknowledged, nonetheless, that "maybe it would be easy for someone to get confused about if they didn't know better." He knew "it would be very sinful" to treat the statue like a pagan idol. Perhaps, he mused, stained-glass windows aren't much different than storybook Bibles.

For Evan and many other young Protestants today, rediscovering the structured worship of a liturgical rite such as a Catholic Mass captured much of the mystery and the receptive posture that he instinctively felt at the well in Ireland. His baptism, when he was about thirteen, was the only other time

Evan had an extraordinary experience which could have been a miracle. Just as he was being baptized, he saw a dove, a sign of the Holy Spirit, fly above him, reinforcing his belief that the Holy Spirit entered his soul at that moment.

Worship focused on the Eucharistic sacrifice, though not a part of Evan's Evangelical faith tradition, is meant to bring the extraordinary into the ordinary. Gestures like kneeling and bowing during Mass, as well as reciting prayers from a sacred text, are all similar to Mary's posture at the Annunciation. Her openness to grace is often depicted as kneeling or bowing in humility, holding the Scriptures that she would have recited daily.

Reconstructing the Faith

Evan's openness to pray to Mary and attend a Eucharistic liturgy like a Catholic Mass was part of a larger journey with that he called a "reconstruction of the faith" that drew on the early church. Having studied engineering as well as classics and history in college, Evan was naturally interested in church history. He lamented how professors at his secular college seemed to deconstruct the faith, upholding a scientific rationalism that denies faith is a part of truth-seeking. Knowing more about church history edified his faith, because "the church has existed through millennia and in different cultures," he said.

Evan's searching to ground his faith by studying church history came in part from disillusionment with certain interactions with some Christians he was close to. After graduating from college, Evan got a job in information technology and worked with a Christian ministry to the poor. But after several years in part-time ministry, he was disillusioned by what he called "church drama." Although the leaders of the ministry agreed on theological questions, personal differences had deteriorated into personal attacks. Sometimes, he lamented that "theology and Scripture were used as a bludgeon."

Although he was attracted to Catholicism's liturgy and sacraments because they freed Sunday worship from the preferences of the local leaders, he nonetheless smiled and said his approach to growing in the faith was "very Protestant," as he had "drunk from many waters at once." For example, Evan studied the Anglican Book of Common Prayer, looking for a structure to connect his scriptural faith to the Nicene Creed, the liturgical calendar, and the history of the saints.

"At a gut level," he said, "when things are hard with other Christians, it's been really helpful to locate my faith with the Nicene Creed." The Nicene Creed is the fundamental statement of Christian faith formulated by the early church councils (primarily at Nicaea in 325 AD) to articulate core Christian doctrines against various heresies that denied the Trinity or the divinity of Christ. Reciting the creed during worship services is meant to unite believers as the body of Christ and expresses in concise language the mysteries of faith about the nature of God and our salvation through Christ.

He lamented "the tendency to politicize the faith," preferring to teach Scripture, serve the poor, and form people's consciences so they engage with the world meaningfully in a variety of ways.

The Feminine in the Church

For Evan, having a woman, Mary, leading him to closer intimacy with God made sense, given his fears about how rationalism had infected both faith and culture. Encountering how Orthodox Christians and Catholics speak of Mary as a nurturing mother did not seem to fall into the stereotypes he had heard from some Christians, such as that women are "warm, fuzzy, and irrational." However, as he put it, "the caricature of the Calvinist conception of God is very rational. If you don't have a nurturing spiritual mother leading you, you get the wrong idea that God is very cold."

Having studied classical civilizations and ancient philosophies, Evan remarked that it is important for society and the church to have masculine and feminine models. "There's a reverent way to be a woman that is necessary for society to function. Similarly, a reverent way of being a man is necessary for society to function."

"What is it like to be a woman?" he asked rhetorically, clarifying that we cannot only answer that question in the abstract. We need concrete examples of men and women to look up to. "It would be unfortunate if there were no archetypes for how to be a woman," he said. "We would end up with the only real archetypes being male. And that would be unfortunate for half of the human race."

He was aware that stereotypes about male and female differences could sometimes be superficial, lamenting that "Evangelicals often don't know a good way to talk about what it means to be feminine." He was careful to explain that speaking of Mary as a role model applied to both men and women. But more than a distant ideal to live up to, Mary represents for Evan a real presence, a mother, a feminine presence in his faith that keeps his heart open to God.

Evan emphasized Mary's spiritual motherhood of the faithful and wished to imitate the love for Mary he saw in his Orthodox and Catholic friends. He chuckled when he recounted how a friend who became Orthodox said that if anyone insulted Mary, it would be like insulting his own mother, and he would punch the offender. "I don't think it's okay to punch people. But that was his way of saying love for Mary is not just some cute little belief. Mary is very vivid to him," as she was now coming closer to Evan, too, as he slowly opened his heart to Mary.

"Hail Mary, Full of Grace, Pray for Us Right Now!"

During another phone conversation a few months later, I asked Evan, "Have you had any other surprising encounters with Mary?"

About a year after visiting the healing well in Ireland, Evan was hiking the Knife's Edge on Mount Katahdin in Maine with a friend. "It was the scariest thing I have ever done. I was tiptoeing, inching hand over hand over this cliff. Death was right in front of me." With the highest peak being 5,269 feet, Mount Katahdin Knife's Edge trail is considered by many to be one of the riskiest in the United States, as hikers must walk along a narrow, exposed ridge. Search-and-rescue missions are common at Mount Katahdin, and fatalities are, unfortunately, not unknown.

"Out of nowhere," Evan recounted with a chuckle, surprised at his own reaction to the fear of death, "I began repeating—Hail Mary, full of grace, pray for us NOW," as he sought safety.

His friend, a lifelong Catholic, was amused by Evan's surprising calls to Mary to send prayers that would save him from death. Once they were safely off the ridge, he couldn't explain to his befuddled friend why he reacted that way. "I don't know why I did it, but that prayer just kept coming to my mind. Even though I probably didn't pray it right, I kept saying it."

My Healing at Lourdes

"Evan, have you heard about the healing waters in Lourdes, France? Or Mary's words to Saint Bernadette there?"

"No, I haven't," he replied.

I was struck by the similarity between the statue and well where Evan was healed in Ireland and those found in Lourdes, France, so I briefly told him the story. In 1858, in the Pyrenees Mountains of Southern France, a young girl named Bernadette Soubirous had several visions of Mary. In one apparition, Mary appeared in blue and white in a grotto and instructed Bernadette to pick up a rock, dig for water, and wash herself with it. When she obeyed, a spring began to flow at that site. Local people flocked to the location and reported miraculous physical healings; soon people from all over France started traveling to Lourdes seeking healing. In 2002, I was one of millions of pilgrims from around the world who visit the healing waters of Lourdes each year.

In the statue at the well in Ireland where Evan stopped to pray, Mary was wearing blue and white, and, like at Lourdes, was standing in a cave, a traditional symbol of Mary's womb that held Christ, where Christ is likened to the unhewn stone that comes from the mountain without human effort (Daniel 2:34 and 2:44–45).

My first trip to Lourdes was in 2002, and it was my first pilgrimage to a significant Marian apparition site. It represented one important step for me out of a rationalistic faith in which I struggled to experience genuine intimacy with God through Mary's motherly intercession.

"Do you reject Satan and all his evil ways?"

"*Oui.*"

"Do you profess your faith in Jesus Christ?"

"*Oui.*"

"Do you wish to be healed of your sins and brought to new life?"

"*Oui.*"

"Now that you have renewed your baptismal promises, you may enter the healing waters."

I leaned backward, falling into the healing waters at the shrine of Our Lady of Lourdes. One, two, three times, the two ladies helped me to lean all the way backwards, submerging my whole body in the well, and repeating each time this three-fold prayer:

"O, Mary, conceived without sin, pray for us. Our Lady of Lourdes, pray for us. Saint Bernadette, pray for us."

When I walked back outside and entered the church for Mass, I wondered: How many people had passed through those gates, gazed at Mary, and brought their hopes, fears, desires, and regrets to her? Around the cave were wheelchairs, crutches, and other objects suggesting that miraculous physical healings had occurred.

At the morning Mass, a couple stood with their daughter, who was confined to a wheelchair. "We first came praying she could walk," they told me after Mass. "She's not had a physical healing, but we feel so spiritually uplifted when we come that we just keep coming back."

I met a religious sister, also alone, and she invited me up the hill to walk the Stations of the Cross, a devotion of fourteen lines from Scripture aimed to help us meditate on Christ's walk to Calvary, from the condemnation of Christ by Pontius Pilate to his bloody crucifixion.

"What brought you to Lourdes?" she asked me.

"Well, I'm feeling very lonely, a bit lost with the direction of my life," I answered. "But I feel like my worries are so little compared to others who come here for physical healings."

"Oh, everyone needs healing, and most of the time it is spiritual," she explained with a caring smile.

In my heart, my burdens felt very trite. What made me worthy of having pious ladies pray with me? I was longing for something I felt unworthy of. But I went through the same ritual again.

Un, deux, trois. Not once, but three times that day, I was submerged in healing waters. Each time, I repeated my baptismal vows: to reject Satan's evil ways, and professed my faith in Christ.

It's not as if I thought three times would bless me more than once, like I could repeat some formula to amplify the result. But the first time I went into the healing waters, I was full of trepidation. I felt awkward as I tried to let go—to let go of myself, my pride, my anger, and my pain.

Un, deux, trois, I laid down all my troubling emotions, my preoccupations, the known and unknown sins, and I made an act of the will, consenting to come home to God through my mother Mary.

Why do millions of people—Catholics as well as Protestants and seekers—go to sites like Lourdes every year? In their book *Image and Pilgrimage in Christian Culture* (1978), cultural anthropologists Victor Turner and Edith Turner showed how pilgrimages in Africa, Europe, and Latin America break through modernity's narrow lenses that have split the spiritual from the material, and the individual from the collective, the personal from the traditional. Pilgrimages are holistic. They entail intense bodily experiences alongside deep mystical encounters with God. Pilgrimages aim for personal growth in one's journey to God while also inviting participants to belong to a community, nation, and ancestors, which have some claim to an authoritative tradition.

That day at Lourdes, I promised God I'd embrace Mary as my spiritual mother. Although Mary had always been present in the churches where I worshiped, like Evan, my personal connection to her was solidified through a deep spiritual experience that felt freeing, uplifting, and that bound me to Christ and his church. However, my specific petition, my personal request that led me to make my first pilgrimage, was not answered in the manner I desperately hoped.

Did that mean that God didn't hear my petition? Perhaps, like Evan, I had imbued a Western, disenchanted worldview and thought that I could memorize doctrines, read Scriptures, follow rules, analyze and then plot out my own path to salvation. But as I plunged into the healing waters at Lourdes,

I realized that we can't predict when or how God might heal us. But his mercy is always reaching out to us. God's healing comes in his time and his way. Going to Lourdes taught me that it's my duty to renounce Satan and profess my faith in Christ while asking for healing and strength.

Just as surely as the ladies held me as I fell backwards into the well, Mary is holding me as I battle to renounce my pride—the greatest sin of all—and open my heart to receive God's grace and submit to his will as Mary did.

Everyday and Extraordinary Graces

Evan's growing sense of Mary's presence alongside him in his journey of faith struck me as a beautiful step to take for a young man whose human virtues and deep faith I admired. Evan's surprising encounter with Mary was one more experience that showed him why a cold rationalism fails to explain human desires for an intimate relationship with God.

Whereas I have grown more comfortable speaking about spiritual experiences as miracles, I respected that Evan wanted to slowly ponder his "wild Marian experience" and mostly sought to imitate Mary's humility and self-effacement rather than proclaim he had experienced a miracle. Evan's insistence that we should seek glory not in exceptional things but in the little things, knowing they all come from God's grace, signified to me a mature faith.

He was right to insist that most of the life of faith is not extraordinary; most of Mary's life was not extraordinary. But I wanted to remind myself that those extraordinary moments, like his wild Marian experience, are a well of strength that can last a lifetime, leading us to ponder new questions and open ourselves to the spirit guiding us.

"Keep pondering, Evan," I wrote to him. "God is leading you somewhere beautiful, that much I know. When the big things come, like your Marian miracle, thank God for your 'old lady friend' named Mary. And if your heart instinctively wants to call Mary for protection and guidance on your journey, I am certain that pleases God."

CHAPTER 3

A Compassionate Witness

Al Raboteau and Mary at the Cross

A Surprising Encounter Spurs a Friendship

"Excuse me, sir, are you Al Raboteau?"

It was a sunny fall day in 2017. While attending daily Mass at St. Paul's Catholic Church in Princeton, New Jersey, I had spotted the esteemed professor of African American Religion kneeling in prayer. I waited outside for him, eager to introduce myself.

I startled him on his way out with my question. "Oh, well, yes I am," he replied, looking puzzled.[1]

"I read your book *Slave Religion* about conversion to Christianity among African American slaves. I saw many parallels to my work on Haitian Catholics, especially about loving one's enemies."

"I'd really like to read your book," he replied. I smiled, pleased at having made a personal connection with a person whose authority in the field of African American Christianity everyone looked up to. I had heard that Al was also a man of deep personal faith, yet I never expected that we would sit a few pews away from each other in prayer.

Sipping coffee one morning in Princeton not long after, I

shared with him how his work had helped me find ways of sharing powerful stories of forgiveness without minimizing the suffering of others.

In the late 1970s, when scholarship on African Americans was greatly expanding, Al's work challenged prior historical understandings that slave conversions to Christianity resulted in passivity to political injustice. Many historians perceived religious belief among slaves as leading to either rebellion or docility. But resistance or accommodation to conditions of slavery were not the only two options, Al argued.

Al was particularly drawn to oral histories of slaves, seeking to recover their voices of suffering and hope, pain and joy. When, in 1978, Al published *Slave Religion: The "Invisible Institution" in the Antebellum South*, he received great acclaim for his beautiful writing that brought to life painful yet hopeful stories from slaves. He hoped to model how the discipline of history can act as a "recovery, a humanistic effort to increase knowledge."[2]

As he wrote in the afterword to an updated edition of *Slave Religion* published twenty-five years after its initial release, "the suffering witness of slave Christians constitutes a major spiritual legacy not only for their descendants but also for any who would take the time to heed the testimony of their words."[3] One of the most controversial things he described in *Slave Religion* was slaves who not only prayed for their masters' conversion but also prayed with their masters. He was criticized for arguing that, despite an asymmetrical power relationship, the "conversion experience of evangelical Christianity created a symbolic common ground" between slave and slave master.[4]

Al argued that conversion of slaves led to a genuine religious reciprocity with their masters,

> whereby blacks and whites preached to, prayed for, and converted each other in situations where the status of master and slave was, at least for the moment, suspended. In the fervor of religious worship, master and slave, white and black, could be found sharing a common event, professing a common faith and experiencing a common ecstasy.[5]

The divine entered their human history, touching their lives intimately and leading to authentic religious conversion among slaves whereby they saw themselves as children of God with an inherent dignity. The conversion experiences of slaves injected new life into them—which, for some, led them to pray for, and sometimes with, their masters.

For instance, Al recounted the story of a slave named Morte who had a profound conversion experience that he shared with his master. His master was so moved that he invited Morte to preach before his household, where Morte spoke about their shared enslavement to sin. Al believed that for Morte, conversion was not merely intellectual; it was felt viscerally in his body. As Al wrote, "people like Morte who have experienced God's total acceptance of them as his children. Conversion changes everything about how they see life, and this change is not only in their head, it's in their body."[6] Their hands and their feet felt new; they were a new creation, body and soul, capable of a love that was previously inconceivable to them, and hard for us today to imagine.

Al feared that when people read *Slave Religion* and he spoke about slaves identifying with the suffering of Jesus, people misunderstood him (and the slaves) as suggesting that believing Jesus is our friend in suffering somehow diminishes the horror of slavery. Rather, Al reminded people that "the suffering of Christ and the martyrs is at the center of the Christian tradition and suffering grounds the Christian to the suffering of the world. As the old slaves knew, suffering can't be evaded, it is a mark of the authenticity of the faith."[7] When asked to name persecuted Christians, he lamented that many people might think of the martyrs of the early church but neglect to think of the persecution of enslaved Christians in America.

To recover the cultural agency of enslaved Christians in America, Al explored the rich tradition of Negro spirituals. This tradition represents what he called an existential grappling with their suffering. He insisted that the musical tradition of enslaved African Americans empowered them, leading to an "acceptance of the sorrow and the joy inherent in the human condition and an affirmation that life in itself was valuable."[8]

Al insisted that historians often overlooked that enslavement did not prevent slaves from exercising "a religious agency of a very real and powerful sort."[9] Slaves' conversion to Christianity truly injected a feeling of new life in them. For the slaves, their African American Christian worship expressed their movement from sorrow to joy, from damnation to elation. What previous work on the conversion of slaves to Christianity had overlooked was that "people who had been through fire and refined like gold reveal the capability of the human spirit not only to endure bitter suffering but also to resist and even transcend the persistent attempt of evil to strike it down."[10]

The paradox enslaved Christians teach us, Al pointed out, is central to Christianity: that suffering can coexist with joy. Al feared that if historians failed to recognize the moral and spiritual dimensions of the slave experience as authentic and liberating, even when their newfound faith did not produce immediate political change, key aspects of the African American Christian tradition would be lost. He hoped that people who read his work would see "the refusal of my people to let injustice strike down their souls and demand their human dignity, the old people's example of gentleness, hospitality, and kindness."[11]

I was one of the people who was deeply inspired by the stories in *Slave Religion*. At our first of many meetings over coffee, I asked Al, "How can I share powerful stories of forgiveness I have heard without diminishing the horror of the evil acts or sound like I'm justifying suffering?"

Holding a copy of my book that he had recently read, Al replied, "You told their stories in their own words, describing how they experience God's presence with them in their suffering." We talked about how too often, scholars like us who earned a PhD in history or sociology, are told to filter human experience through abstract categories like power that reduces all human agency to the political realm. "But," Al insisted, "it's also the task of a scholar to faithfully present people's stories in all their complexity, including their encounters with God in the midst of tribulation. If we just apply our theories to stories and erase their words, we risk taking away people's own moral voices when those very voices might challenge us."

Al Finds Refuge in Mary's Motherhood

The more I got to know Al in the following years, the more I realized that, like me, hearing about others' experiences of suffering and forgiveness had profoundly affected his own practice of the Chrsitian faith, including his drawing nearer to Mary when he desperately needed forgiveness and compassion.

Born in the 1940s to a Catholic family in Louisiana and descended from slaves, Al knew personally that the evils of slavery had continued in the US through segregation and racism. At the same time, Al was a fervent Catholic throughout his young adulthood. He attended Mass regularly and served as an altar boy. As a young man, Al loved liturgy and theology and considered becoming a Catholic priest. But his love for writing led him first to shift his focus to English literature as an undergraduate at the University of California at Berkeley. When the Civil Rights Movement began, Al felt a call to serve promote justice through his scholarship, going to Yale University to pursue a PhD in history.

At Princeton University, Al quickly ascended to influential positions, including Dean of Princeton's Graduate School. But something wasn't right. In his spiritual memoir *A Sorrowful Joy: A Spiritual Memoir of an African-American Man in Late Twentieth-Century America*, Al shared that his meteoric rise to academic prestige had come at a significant personal cost. He felt resentful, terribly unhappy. The religious rituals he once enjoyed felt like a burden. He held on to perfectionism and guilt but not a living faith. He looked for joy in aesthetic experiences, but they eventually became empty. The love for God he had once felt was nearly extinguished. His reputation soared, but his soul wandered in a desert.

In this spiritual desert, he had an affair. He and his wife divorced. Very quickly after his marriage ended, he lamented the harm he had done to his wife and children, describing how, "I started an earthquake that only God could stop, and the damage to several lives was devastating. It got so bad that every morning I would throw up. I couldn't stomach the mess I had made of my life . . . my spirit was bleeding all over the place."[12]

Seeking some sort of anchor to return to faith, Al attended an art exhibition at the Princeton University Art Museum called "Gates of Mystery: Sacred Art of Russia." He was so enraptured by an icon of the Virgin Mary, the *Theotokos*, that he returned three times to look upon the icon. Her face, her eyes, and her real presence with him in his longing for God gave him hope that not all was lost. Contemplating that image of Mary, he, too, came to believe he could experience mercy and healing. "She seemed to hold all the hurt in the world with those eyes. I stood in front of her for a long time. I gazed at her, and she gazed at me."[13]

Following this mystical encounter with Mary, Al went to an Eastern Orthodox liturgy. The candles, the incense, and the hymns all spoke to him of God's real but veiled presence in the world. Mary, and the faces of all the saints, were for Al living members of the church, now united with God, reaching out to him. The face of Mary had moved him so deeply: she was as real to him as his own family, whose pictures dotted his home.

Longing to come home to God, Al described how "I felt the presence of generations of Christians standing with us, generations moving into the Church with us: martyrs, confessors, our ancestors in the faith . . . so many hands holding me up."[14] Mary's maternal love seemed to be able to hold on both the joy and sorrow in Al's heart as he pleaded with God for inner peace.

To keep that powerful spiritual experience alive in his daily life, Al created a sacred space in his home, an icon corner where he prayed by the light of an oil lamp. "I kept it lit against the darkness without and the darkness within," he wrote.[15] Shortly thereafter, he visited an Eastern Orthodox monastery and cried repentantly, begging for God's mercy, repeating countless times a short prayer called the Jesus Prayer, "Lord Jesus Christ, Son of God, have mercy on me, a sinner."

Al made another pilgrimage not too long after, this one to Assisi, Italy. He prayed before the cross of San Damiano where St. Francis of Assisi had a powerful spiritual experience in 1205, hearing and heeding God's call to rebuild his church. Al knelt before the cross of San Damiano, knowing his fervent repentance for his failings was leading him to a renewed commitment to the Christian faith.

Mary had been so central to Al's return to faith that after returning from his pilgrimages, Al worked with a few others to bring an Orthodox Church to Princeton, naming the church for the *Theotokos*, the Mother of God. He explained the choice to dedicate the church to Mary by quoting an ancient hymn, "The Joy of All Who Sorrow."

Joy of all who sorrow art thou,
protectress of the oppressed,
feeder of the hungry,
consolation of travelers,
haven for The Tempest tossed,
visitation of the sick,
protection and aid of the infirm,
Staff of old age,
O, all pure Mother of the Most High God,
hasten, we pray, to save thy servants.[16]

For Al, the "joy of all who sorrow" was more than a theoretical idea. Al always felt personally called to shine the light of hope into the lives of those who experience profound suffering. Now, Mary's motherhood became a refuge for him, where her strength and her tenderness gave him hope and courage to continue sharing Christian love with the suffering as Mary does.

Mary experienced spiritual martyrdom at the cross. She willingly watched her son's gruesome death and did not abandon him. God does not always prevent worldly suffering. But the Christian message of redemptive suffering, which Al wrote about, does not mean that we sit by passively in the face of injustice. Compassion with those who suffer unjustly can create a new family, a bond of love that is greater than worldly evil.

Standing at the Foot of the Cross

From the cross, Jesus called those standing by him in his final moments to behold his mother. In John 19:25–27, Scripture tells us:

> But standing by the cross of Jesus were his mother, and his mother's sister, Mary, the wife of Clopas, and Mary Magdalene. When Jesus saw his mother, and the disciple whom he loved standing near, he said to his mother: "Woman, behold your son!" Then, he said to the disciple, "Behold your mother." And from that hour, the disciple took her to his own home.

In this moment on the cross, Jesus signifies that the shedding of his blood has created a new spiritual reality: a communion we can experience with one another through Jesus. United by his sacrifice on the cross, we are each other's spiritual family, capable of a love refined through suffering.

Most of the disciples deserted Jesus during his passion. By standing as a witness to Christ's brutal death, Mary and John embody how we cannot avoid the cross. By uniting themselves with Christ in his sufferings, they participate in the divine life: a love that sacrifices itself for others.

Mary bore her son's pain in her heart as deeply as any mother would who watches her son die. Mary's compassion for her son is a natural response to a mother witnessing the horror of his death by crucifixion. Her compassion was not an act of resignation or passivity but rather one of spiritual martyrdom. Mary trusted that God would bring glory even from the horrific crucifixion she witnessed.

Remembering Mary's presence at the foot of the cross through art, songs, and rituals provides embodied ways we learn to imitate her compassion in our lives. Mary's compassion with the suffering is not just something of the past; it was her compassion for him that Al felt deep inside his heart at the art exhibit that gave him the courage to throw himself at the feet of Jesus and beg for mercy when he had upended his family life. Al dedicated his career—especially after his personal return to a deeper faith—to spreading this message of forgiveness and mercy.

"How often we don't see moments of love," Al lamented. It's understandable that "the pain, the injustice, the abuse, and the evil—passing on generation after generation—blind us."[17] But, he wrote, gently encouraging others in their faith, "if we search, we can see that our compassion conveys God's love." Importantly, Al noted that our cooperation is required, noting that "it is through us, *if we permit it* [emphasis mine], that God reaches out to heal our wounds. It is through our love for one another that he transforms our sadness into joy."[18]

The Gospel testimony that Mary stood at the foot of the cross reminds us that we cannot always prevent suffering, and we too, like Mary did for Jesus, can offer a gaze, a presence, a spiritual embrace. Mary's compassionate eyes helped Al personally to see "how much God loves each of us at every instant and that it was God's love certainly not our perfection that matters."[19] Mary's compassion for Al, Al's compassion for others, all point to a love that knows no bounds or limits—God's love.

As Al wrote in *Slave Religion*, Christianity is not a religion that loves suffering as if suffering itself is the good. Rather, Christianity proclaims that that the love of God is bigger than even cruel suffering. In his zeal to spread this message of hope, Al came to understand more deeply what had happened to him when he encountered Mary's gaze. Her compassion, her love expressed in the hymn "The Joy of All Who Sorrow," had been the mirror that reflected God's love pouring out to him when he embarked on his return home to faith.

Radical Forgiveness

In 2015, Al gave a talk on forgiveness in the African American church experience at the Faith Angle Forum, which brings together scholars and journalists from religious and secular backgrounds. He opened the talk by reading three Scripture passages about forgiveness and loving one's enemies: The Lord's Prayer from Matthew Chapter 6:12, in which Jesus teaches us to ask our Father forgive us "as we also have forgiven"; Jesus's exhortation in Matthew 5:44 to "Love your enemies and pray for those who persecute you"; and Jesus's words from the cross in Luke 23:34, "Father, forgive them for they know not what they do."

After quoting Scripture three times, he then named, one by one, each of the victims of the racially motivated shooting in 2015 at the historic Emanuel African Methodist Episcopal Church in Charleston, South Carolina. Al reflected on their family members who forgave the killer, shocking many people. To place their actions in context, Al encouraged those present to reflect on the history of the African American church in America, including powerful stories he had written about, such as Morte's, who had forgiven his master and even prayed for him and with him.

At the end of the presentation, a journalist challenged Al's interpretation of redemptive suffering among slaves as being a powerful way that—albeit across time—the American nation could grow closer to its ideals. If forgiveness didn't change the fact that they were still slaves, doesn't that just mean their religion made them passive?

Al responded vigorously to the challenge, speaking with the certainty of someone who has received the same question about his work for decades.

> But they are not *just* slaves . . . that's not their only reality. They are children of God with spiritual power. Don't forget Exodus. Their enslavement is not forever. Their children's slavery will come to an end because God intervenes in human history to cast down the mighty and lift up the lowly. . . . Maybe it's not a plot for revolt, but it is revolutionary action regarding what matters most. Who is the most important source of value in my life? It's God, not the Master.[20]

Al knew that his words challenged not only people who thought of themselves as secular, but also some Christians who wished to distance themselves from the radical call to love one's enemies that he had quoted from Scripture. Al acknowledged that the slaves' experiences and words simply do not make sense apart from a firm belief in the supernatural reality they believed in: namely, that Christ had died on the cross for our sins, and our acts of forgiveness unleash divine power in the world.

When Al visited a class I taught on religion, resilience, and vulnerability at Princeton Theological Seminary and delivered the same lecture on forgiveness in the African American church tradition, he faced a similar question from a student:

Doesn't forgiving one's enemies detract from political action promoting justice?

As all the students in that class were baptized Christians studying theology, he challenged them to ask themselves if they believed *all* of the Gospel. "If you pray the Lord's Prayer, you say, 'Forgive us our trespasses as we forgive those who trespass against us.' If you don't believe those words, then stop praying the Lord's Prayer," he said.

Al's words were a challenge to all listening to probe their conscience and ask: Are any of us worthy of the forgiveness we all need? How many times had I asked God for forgiveness yet was still tempted to refuse that forgiveness to those who have harmed me?

As we walked across campus after that encounter, I remarked to Al that the his examples taught me that to name one's oppressors, to name the harm done, and then hand it over to God is a form of justice because it acknowledges the evil done, thus making a moral judgment. By leaving the punishment to God, hoping for repentance and conversion rather than more suffering, forgiveness is also an act of charity. "You are right, that's what the Gospel teaches, and it's not humanly possible. But with God, all things are possible."

Forgiving the Unforgiveable

Sipping a coffee in New York City in 2019, the woman next to me asked, "What brings you to Manhattan?"

Nervously, I answered, "I'm here to share stories about people who forgive others for acts of violence."

After a few seconds of heavy silence, she shared a story of

a friend who had forgiven a man who broke into her apartment, stole from her, and beat her. She was clearly both troubled and inspired by her friend's choice to forgive.

Later that night, as I shared the stage at Columbia University with a philosophy professor, we discussed the ethics of forgiveness at an event sponsored by The Veritas Forum. Is there anything special about the Christian approach to forgiveness? Can we reason our way to forgive others without religious faith, simply because it's good for the social fabric and to reduce our own anxiety?

In that large public forum, I did not avoid making a point that many find troubling and others find inspiring: that forgiveness of one's enemies is much more than a rationally calculated choice to improve one's own well-being or that of society. Following Al's example, I tried to bring together my personal need for forgiveness with others' stories about radical acts of forgiveness.

One story I shared that night at Columbia University came from my research among Haitian Catholics. I'll never forget one woman, Stephanie, who I met when I was helping tutor an English class at Notre Dame d'Haiti Catholic Church in Miami. She was always joyful and walked around sharing with others a poem about love. One day while sitting in the courtyard of the church, I asked her why she left Haiti. She told me a horrible story. One day, a group of thugs broke into her house and raped her, burning her car as they left.

After telling me her painful story, she wiped her tears and a look of joy came over her face. She then described how these horrible experiences didn't change what she had been taught in her Catholic school in Haiti: to love everyone, even those with more money, or from other racial or ethnic groups, even those who are your enemies. I was truly astounded, however, when Stephanie told me she prayed for the men who raped her.

Stephanie insisted that "people who do bad things, like the people who burned my car, they know when they are doing something wrong. So it is up to God to touch their hearts and change them. If someone hurts you, you have to pray for them. If someone hates you, you have to love them."[21]

In sociology or psychology I often found explanations of forgiveness in terms of the psychological benefits to oneself, or even in terms of social harmony. But Stephanie's ability to forgive came not from a choice to comply with a burdensome obligation for the good of society, but as a freely given response to having received God's gifts of love and mercy herself. She trusted that God would change their hearts and, if they would acknowledge their wrongs, he would offer his mercy.

There was a time when I wondered if such forgiveness is due to the unrepentant. But hearing from Stephanie and others who had experienced horrific acts of violence and yet forgave people, even if they had not knowingly repented, revealed something profound to me. Christ's death on the cross, not our righteousness nor the repentance of those who harm us, is what allows for us to be reconciled with God.

That night at Columbia University, I remarked that maybe those of us who teach at Ivy League universities, who don't have to struggle to survive, can discuss the ethics of justice and the benefits of forgiving one's enemies for self and society. But the lives of women like Stephanie and the slaves whom Al wrote about speak eloquently the language of the heart of faith in Christ's redemption, which opens the possibility of forgiveness for all.

What I have seen when I visited war zones, and when I interviewed women in the US and in Haiti who have been victims of violence, is that they are *moved* to forgive by a power bigger than themselves. They don't read an academic treatise on justice and choose forgiveness from a menu of options. The spirit moves them first. Their choice is much more than the exercise of an independent, autonomous free will seeking maximum personal benefit. It's an expression of spiritual freedom, a gift from God.

That night at Columbia, I said emphatically, echoing Al's words, that radical stories of forgiveness are meant to be a witness that challenges us, changes us, and moves us. If we are blinded and refuse to see such actions as a witness to a divine power, then we may miss an opportunity to let others' compassionate courage reveal to us the divine at work in history.

In a reflection I published shortly afterwards, I responded to a question I often get: How realistic is it to expect such courageous acts of forgiveness? The pain caused by violent crime and intentional evil leaves deep wounds. But the Christian faith, and the heroic examples of innocent people who suffer and yet love their enemies, proclaims that the human heart can love, grow, and expand even under conditions of oppression. This is not a sentimental love; it is a love that seeks charity in truth, in justice, and in regarding our neighbor who has harmed us as a person deserving of the same merciful love that we ourselves have already been shown.

Theologian Robert Schreiter explains forgiveness as stemming from the desire of a heart that wants to expand. Schreiter explains a few principles from the Christian tradition that help facilitate forgiveness and reconciliation. First, God is the author of reconciliation. God initiates reconciliation and gives us the freedom to participate (or not) in it. Second, justice for evil we experience may never happen in our lives but can happen beyond our lifetime. For Christians, however, reconciliation, restoration, and healing begin now with God's acting in the victim's life in the present moment. Third, reconciliation means that God can save the wrongdoer *and* the victim, making new creations of both. Fourth, through private devotions and public rituals, Christians lodge their own sufferings in the story of the suffering and death of Christ. The fifth point Schreiter makes is that reconciliation will not be complete until God is all in all. For a Christian, hope is eschatological and reconciliation is cosmic. Hope is not bound by the limits of time and is not ultimately destroyed by the dysfunction of the human heart.[22]

Although Mary did not speak at the foot of the cross, her presence, her witness reminds us that we are not alone if we struggle to see the divine at work in our suffering. The tender love of a mother can hold us, preparing us to receive the grace of a peaceful heart—that interior freedom that Jesus wants to give us even as we bear our crosses in this world, with the assurance that his kingdom is here with us now, albeit imperfectly. Together, we can walk toward that time when his kingdom is all in all, with love and hope.

Al's kind eyes, his gentle voice, and his presence radiated love. Al's encounter with Mary through art, liturgy, music, and private prayer was deeply intimate: he felt her presence guiding him, her holiness was radiating into him and helped him heal. Her tender love can reach us in our darkest moments and renew our hope.

Pray for the Suffering[23]

Tears streamed down my cheeks as I placed my right hand over Al's hand. A few days earlier, his wife had called to let me know that Al's battle with terminal illness was coming to an end.

That day in 2021, I drove to Al's house for one final conversation with him. Covered in a quilt with "Grandpa" stitched on it, my collaborator and fellow sojourner in faith struggled to keep his eyes open. My voice cracked as I promised Al that I would continue teaching his books, especially his 1978 classic, *Slave Religion: The Invisible Institution and Antebellum Slavery*. I thanked him for so many mornings of coffee at Halo Pub after daily Mass at St. Paul's Catholic Church in Princeton, where we discussed our shared passion for exploring human experiences of the divine.

Knowing we shared a deep love for Mary, I showed him three sacred objects I had brought: an icon of Mary that I purchased in Cyprus, a pocket oratory with reproductions of four icons painted by my husband, David, and a rosary someone had given me when I wept over the death of a former student of mine named John.

Al struggled to speak, but after I showed him each object, he replied in his gentle voice, "Thank you. That's beautiful."

Then, I put my hand on his shoulder and chanted all of Psalm 51:1–3 in English, which begins:

> Have mercy upon me, O God, according to thy steadfast love; according to thy abundant mercy, blot out my transgressions. Wash me thoroughly from my iniquity, and cleanse me from my sin. For I know my transgressions, and my sin is ever before me.

When I finished, I asked, "How can I pray for you, Al?"

"Pray for others. Pray for the suffering," he replied softly.

Slowly, Al lifted his hand and placed it on mine. I leaned over and kissed his forehead. Then, I said three Hail Marys aloud by his bedside and departed.

I drove away from Al's house and allowed tears to flow freely as I prayed the rosary, imploring Mary to accompany Al in his final days and to teach me to be compassionate with all those who suffer.

Al passed away a few days later at the age of seventy-eight. Shortly after, as at every Orthodox funeral, we chanted hymns imploring God's mercy on Al's soul and implored Mary to welcome him to eternal glory.

CHAPTER 4

A Tear in the World

Sally's Life-Saving Encounter with Mary

The Woman in Blue

One day in 2023, I received an email from a woman named Sally who had heard about my love of Mary from an older woman who had mentored her at her United Methodist Church. In her email to me, she explained that she had been raised without a religious faith and had entered a Protestant church as a young adult. Having read my article about a pilgrimage to Fátima, Portugal, in which I wrote about my grief after the death of a former student,[1] she felt comfortable making a startling revelation with me over email that she had not shared with many people:

"Mary saved my life. I'd like to share my story with you."

When we connected not long afterwards over Zoom, I saw an attractive young woman in her late twenties on the screen. She appeared nervous, her voice trembling as she opened the conversation, remarking, "I have never desired anything as much as I long to be a mother."

After getting married in her mid-twenties, she had suffered two miscarriages in close succession. She described how her dreams of motherhood were met with grueling bodily pain and indescribable sadness. But Sally went on to describe how, in the midst of her agony, she had a series of mystical experiences which not only consoled her but also unveiled a new way of understanding her faith in Jesus and her relationship to his mother, Mary.

She pleaded with me, “I’m not asking you to believe what I am about to tell you. But please hold what I say with open hands. I decided to trust you with this story because I know Mary is real to you. Mary’s presence felt very real to me, too.”

Sally then described a mysterious vision she had one night when she awoke from a dream. Not wanting to wake up her husband, she walked to her living room and laid down on the couch. She vividly recalled that moment when, suddenly, looking up at the ceiling, it seemed as though a tear had formed in the world.”

She searched for words to describe this vision, adding, “Through the tear, I could see a woman with dark hair dressed in blue, floating above an ocean at night. Stars twinkled faintly in the distance.” My heart leapt when she provided details which we discussed later that clearly connected this woman to Mary: “The woman wore a deep blue-green veil adorned with stars draped over her head and arms.”

Initially, Sally thought she was dreaming. She fell asleep on the couch, and when she got up in the morning, she took a shower. When she walked out of her room, she had a second vision. “Mary stood in the hallway, floating again through a tear in the world.” As if to describe Mary connecting heaven and earth, Sally noted how, “stars twinkled faintly behind her as ocean waves rolled silently below her feet.”

Raptured in attention, Sally recounted, “I stood in silence, not sure what to do, when I felt Mary communicate with me. Wordlessly, she somehow made it known to me that, if my husband and I were open to life, I would conceive."

Given her strong desire to be a mother and the miscarriages she had faced, Sally received this message with a bit of trembling. "I also felt a sadness and a weight with her message. If we conceived a child, I had the sense it wouldn't end well."

She wrestled in her heart with whether she would open her heart and body to the risk of another pregnancy with no guarantees. Fear gripped her heart. "Trying to conceive again after a second miscarriage feels like believing in a miracle, with a real possibility of being stabbed to death," she said. "There's no way to prepare for the heartbreak of another miscarriage."

But Sally couldn't shake the sense that Mary's maternal presence meant something, no matter what happened. Sally sensed that this astonishing message from Mary was not commanding her what to do. Mary had called on her, but how she would respond to the message was not immediately clear to her.

"I felt like Mary was inviting me to step into something that was a part of God's plan," she told me. Although fear gripped her as she pondered the risk of losing yet another baby, she also believed that "the Mother of God wouldn't have come here to tell me I might conceive a child again soon if it didn't mean something important."

Sally shared her hopes and fears with her husband. Despite the risk, they agreed to be open to conceiving a new life.

Indeed, as Mary had indicated, Sally and her husband

conceived a baby that month. But Sally's joy at the life growing in her was tempered by fears of another miscarriage. As with her previous pregnancies, her body showed signs that something was wrong. Terrified of experiencing another heartbreaking loss, Sally pleaded with Mary to intercede on her behalf and let her baby live.

Despite her fervent pleas, Sally grew more anxious. She sensed in her body that, yet another time, her pregnancy had ended in a miscarriage. She went to the doctor and requested an ultrasound. The bad news crushed her dreams once again.

There was no heartbeat. No yolk sac. Her womb was empty, the doctor said.

The devastating news barely had time to sink before Mary appeared to Sally again. "This time," Sally recalled, "her countenance was grave." In a few days, Sally was about to board a six-hour flight and move with her husband to start a new career. Mary's solemn gaze indicated to Sally that something had to be wrong. Although Mary did not speak to her audibly, "Mary clearly communicated to me that I should *not* fly," Sally insisted.

Sally pleaded with the doctor for another ultrasound. Could she still be carrying her baby inside her womb?

This time the analysis was different, and it confirmed that Mary's warning was not in vain. Although there was no baby in Sally's womb, her tiny baby was alive in her fallopian tube. In this situation, known as an ectopic pregnancy, there is no chance for the baby's ultimate survival in that location, though for a few weeks, the baby can live and grow inside the mother's fallopian tube. In such a situation, the mother faces great risk: if the tube bursts, she could bleed to death.

The doctors told Sally that if she gone through with her plans to fly such a long distance, the change in air pressure would likely have caused her ectopic pregnancy to rupture. The bleeding would be so severe that there would not have been time to land the plane and rush her to a hospital. Had she flown and had her tube burst, both Sally and the baby would have perished.

Sadly, and painfully, as with almost every ectopic pregnancy, the baby ultimately died. But, with the agony of her loss still in her voice, Sally nonetheless firmly asserted, "Mary saved my life."

To Sally, her body, instead of being a sanctuary where new life was protected so it could grow, had turned into a vessel for the deaths of three children in succession. In the following months, Sally was unsure if she belonged to the land of the living or the realm of the dead. Although she was not to blame, her shame was so deep that she tried to avoid approaching others in public, fearing her body's apparent curse might harm innocent strangers.

Sally paused, perhaps trying to read my face to see my reaction. I could barely fathom the tremendous loss she had endured. I knew I could not take away her pain, yet I knew Sally had sought me out because she wanted to hear my insights on Mary's motherhood, especially for those who have endured such painful losses.

I stared at the image of Mary on my desk and rubbed my hands on my rosary beads, lifting Sally up in prayer. I asked Mary to help me find words to say to this sad young woman she had visited.

Then I took a deep breath and tried as hard as one can

to connect personally with someone over Zoom. I looked directly into her sad eyes and held her gaze as long as I could while sharing my conviction that the woman she had seen in the tear in the world was, indeed, Mary, the Mother of God. Then, hoping to strengthen her faith in eternal life, the only possible spiritual consolation after losing three children, I firmly stated: "I'm sure Mary wants you to know that your children are with her in heaven."

Then, no longer able to choke back my tears, I added, "Mary wants you to know that you will see your children one day, and they will recognize you as their mother."

Sally nodded her head and slowly replied, "Thank you for speaking about my children as though they are people."

It broke my heart to think that any mother might wonder if a child who died inside of her body was lost forever in some impersonal void.

I could scarcely fathom the sense of loss she described, yet in my mind, she was already a mother, but separated painfully from her children. I had no doubt that the children who had been in Sally's womb were now in heaven and that they would be reunited one day with her.

Such an assurance of eternal life, however, does not automatically take away the pain. I sensed that Mary's maternal presence could continue to embrace Sally's wounds with love.

"You are not alone," I assured her. "Mary understands your sorrow."

Mary as the New Eve

Several months later, Sally and I met in person for the first time. Over dinner together, she shared more about her teenage conversion to Christianity that had come from a deep desire to connect to something eternal and sacred. Although she was accomplished in her career and had many professional opportunities, she remarked that her greatest desire in life was "to raise a child on this side of heaven."

As she had seen visions of Mary, I opened the conversation talking about artistic images of Mary.

One particular image had come to mind when she shared her story. Although not identical, the woman Sally had seen resembled the same descriptions of Mary in Scripture that were echoed in the accounts of her 1531 appearance to an Aztec named Juan Diego on Tepeyac Hill in present-day Mexico City.

"Before your vision, had you ever seen an image of Our Lady of Guadalupe?" I asked.

"No," she replied. Prior to Mary's appearances to her, Sally had not learned much about her at all. "At my church," she remarked, "except for Christmas, we rarely discuss Mary. It's like we celebrate the birth of Christ and then forget his mother."

The resonance between her vision and Our Lady of Guadalupe had immediately struck me, as Our Lady of Guadalupe is often associated with Mary protecting pregnant women. The origin of this particular image of Mary stems from Mary's appearance in 1531 to the Aztec Juan Diego. Mary had appeared to him as an Aztec woman would have looked. She had dark hair with a central parting, signifying her virginity. The ribbon around her waist indicated she was pregnant. Her robe had eight-pointed stars on it, a traditional symbol connecting Mary to Christ, who rose on the eighth day of the week. The image of Our Lady of Guadalupe convinced the Spanish Archbishop of the authenticity of Juan Diego's visions because the upturned crescent moon on the bottom of the image resembled the image of the woman described in the Book of Revelation.

"Have you read about the description of the woman in the Book of Revelation," I asked Sally, "who is thought by many to be an allegorical description of Mary?" Revelation 12:1 describes how "a great sign appeared in heaven: a woman clothed with the sun, with the moon under her feet and a crown of twelve stars on her head." The next verse describes the woman as being pregnant and crying out in childbirth.

I hoped that discussing the image of Our Lady of Guadalupe and the Scripture verse from Revelation might deepen Sally's sense that Mary can walk with us through this valley of tears until we are reunited with our loved ones. After her visions, Sally had begun to read about Mary and had learned about Our Lady of Guadalupe and the symbolism associated with her image. But reading about Mary was not enough. She wanted to share her story with me because, as she put it, "This isn't just theoretical to me. And I know Mary is real to you."

Sitting at my kitchen table and opening her heart more to me, Sally shared her sense of abandonment and rage.

"I felt abandoned in my flesh. Even if my body was alive, my soul felt dead."

However, she continued, "even if I will never fully understand, I knew God was still with me in this somehow. If the Mother of God had appeared to me, I somehow knew that, even if I felt no spiritual consolation, God was still there."

Because she felt that her experiences of loss as a mother somehow mirrored Mary's suffering as a mother, Sally opened her heart to Mary.

"At that moment, if a man had appeared to me, even Jesus," she said somewhat incredulously but sincerely, "I'm not sure I would have opened my heart. But this was Jesus's *mother* who appeared to me."

Humbly, and gently, Sally added, "I hesitate to compare myself to Mary. But knowing Mary had experienced unspeakable grief at the death of her son made me feel less alone. Mary's presence made me feel seen—as if she witnessed my suffering and my hopes."

Sally is not what she calls a "silver-linings Christian," someone who is always looking to put a positive spin on everything. Her painful losses are tragic. But she acknowledged that in seeing Mary, pondering Mary's suffering, and opening her heart to Mary, "Mary helped me let go of some of my rage."

Sally and I discussed how, although it is natural to pray to God for relief from our suffering, the Christian faith does not shy away from the cross. God's love is stronger than the pain of our losses. God did not abandon us in our suffering—while on the cross, Jesus left us his mother to be our mother, too. The Christian Gospel does not tell us that we will be free from suffering. But neither do we have to face suffering all alone—we have a mother in heaven who reaches out to us, consoling us. As painful as it is to lose a loved one, Sally and I discussed that the sense we have that we will one day be reunited with our loved ones in a restored paradise can transform our tears of sorrow into a joyful anticipation of renewed life in Christ.

Apart from continued visions, which Sally did not expect nor ask for, how might Sally form a picture in her mind of Mary as a gateway to a restored paradise? Sally's relationship with Mary had begun with a series of powerful visions, and I believed that sacred art could help connect her visions back to the hopeful message of our salvation told in the Scriptures. Sacred images often are able to portray a paradox such as hope in eternal life better than words alone.

Since my husband is an artist, sacred images adorn our home and art books populate our library. I showed Sally a book about Fra Angelico (the "Angelic Friar"), born Guido di Pietro around 1395 in Vicchio, Italy, who was a friar of the Dominican Order (the Order of Preachers) and one of the most celebrated artists of the fifteenth century, whose work is admired widely today. In the same monasteries where his fellow Dominican, St. Thomas Aquinas, had lived and worked centuries before him, Fra Angelico painted the walls with frescoes of various scenes from the Scriptures. The significance of the Annunciation is underscored by the fact that Christian artists have painted it more than any other Gospel scene—including the Nativity.

Sally and I looked at one of Fra Angelico's famous images of the Annunciation, shown on page 70, which depicts the biblical scene with delicate colors, graceful figures, and gold leaf embellishments. His painting includes details not in Scriptures but often depicted in art. We talked about how, in this painting, we saw both Mary on the right and the Archangel Gabriel to her left, bowing with arms crossed as a sign of respect and humility. At the top left of the painting, one of the cherubim is expelling the distressed Adam and

Eve from the Garden of Eden. In Scripture, Christ is called the new Adam (1 Corinthians 15:45–47), and early church fathers such as Irenaeus and Justin Martyr (140–200) called Mary the New Eve. In Genesis, Eve's cooperation with the serpent turned her away from God, causing the fall, the breach between humankind and God symbolized by our expulsion from the Garden of Eden. Fra Angelico added this detail to the Annunciation to contrast Mary's "yes," her free consent to God's will, with Eve's refusal to do God's will.

To remind viewers of Mary's presence throughout the Gospels, below the main image of the Fra Angelico painting of the Annunciation are scenes from Mary's life: her marriage to Joseph, her visit to her cousin Elizabeth, the birth of Christ, the Presentation of Christ in the Temple after forty days, and Mary's Assumption into heaven. Beyond the literal depiction of the historical event, the painting moves into the symbolic interpretation of the Scriptures around the Annunciation.

"Each word at the Annunciation is ripe with meaning that the artist is trying to capture in this painting," I said. Sally and I then discussed the Scriptures from Luke that describe the Annunciation.

Luke tells us that Mary did not know how the great mystery of bearing a child could happen. Luke tells us that Mary was "greatly troubled" by the angel's greeting: "Hail, full of grace, the Lord is with you" (Luke 1: 28–29). When the angel then said she will bear a child who will be called "the Son of Most High . . . and he will reign over the house of Jacob forever" (Luke 1:32–33), Mary asks the angel: "How can this be, since I have no husband?" (Luke 1:34).

The angel then promises Mary that "the Holy Spirit will

By Fra Angelico—Own work, CC BY-SA 4.0, https://commons.wikimedia.org/w/index.php?curid=125056530.

come upon you, and the power of the Most High will overshadow you." (Luke 1:35). To demonstrate that "nothing will be impossible with God" (Luke 1:37), the angel tells Mary that Elizabeth, her cousin thought to be barren, would bear a child in her old age. Luke (1:38) then tells us that Mary replied to the angel, "Behold, I am the handmaid of the Lord. Let it be done to me according to your word."

"Mary may not speak much in Scripture," I said to Sally, "but Luke made sure to record Mary's initial fear and how her hesitation was transformed into her consent. She believed the Holy Spirit would give her the strength to follow God's plan, even if she didn't know what would come next."

I explained to Sally that I had picked up the Catechism of the Catholic Church—the summary of the Church's beliefs and practices—to see how it addresses Mary. In paragraph 494, the Catechism discusses Mary's "obedience of faith" and states that her consent was necessary for God's plan to be fulfilled. The Catechism then quotes the church fathers, noting that "St. Irenaeus says, 'Being obedient she became the cause of salvation for herself and for the whole human race. . . . The knot of Eve's disobedience was untied by Mary's obedience: what the virgin Eve bound through her disbelief, Mary loosened by her faith.'"[2]

Fra Angelico invites us to ponder the meaning of this profound comparison the church fathers made: Eve's cooperation with the serpent had turned her away from God, causing the fall, the mark of sin we all bear. Mary's free "yes" at the Annunciation allowed God to enter the world in the person of Jesus, marking a whole new beginning for humankind. By comparing Mary to Eve, the church fathers and Fra Angelico remind us just how much God respects our freedom: God does not impose his will on us. Mary's body formed a bridge through which God entered human history; her free consent formed a spiritual bridge reconnecting human nature with divine grace.

I also shared with Sally a copy of an article I wrote about Mary's obedience at the Annunciation.[3] In that article, I reflected on how philosophers such as Charles Taylor and Alasdair MacIntyre have written that one of the key elements of modernity is understanding freedom as autonomy.

Dependence is rejected, and self-expression is exalted. Many feminists such as Judith Butler have written that women's liberation requires rejecting social roles, including motherhood.

Despite coming from a secular background and having countless opportunities to pursue a high-powered career, Sally's deep desires for motherhood were instinctive to her and infinitely more important than her career. Nothing in this world could compete with Sally's desire to be a mother. Sally had given her whole heart, body, and soul not once, but three times in the hopes of becoming a mother. She had embraced a total dependence, a risk to her own life, in the hopes of carrying a child from conception to birth. Was her experience somehow meaningless, something she could discard in pursuit of her true happiness—autonomy? Clearly not in her mind.

The more Sally learned about Mary's freedom at the Annunciation, the more she believed that "my choice to trust was meaningful to God." Although she feared that if she got pregnant again, she would suffer even more, she nonetheless felt that "I was invited to be a part of something I didn't understand, and I trusted enough to risk it."

The *Annunciation* painting and its literal and symbolic interpretations were particularly intriguing to Sally. She remarked that God's power to perform such a miraculous act as the Incarnation had previously led her to believe that Mary's role in Christ's birth was largely passive. But having lost three pregnancies, she now understood that a mother can never simply be a passive vessel for a new life.

Although Sally still hesitated to compare herself to Mary, she realized that Mary's cooperation with God's meant that, at the Incarnation, Mary literally gave human flesh to Jesus, who retained his divinity. Even though she had lost three babies before birth, Sally could see a parallel between her experience of motherhood and Mary's, in that "we are all invited to be a part of something God is doing. Faith without knowing how the story ends is important to God."

Acknowledging Mary's free consent at the Annunciation does not lessen the miraculous conception of Jesus, which occurred through extraordinary grace, she said. But looking at this painting and pondering her experience, Sally could now see how God's grace is a gift that we are free to accept or reject. The misuse of human freedom led Eve to turn away from God in the Garden of Eden. Recognizing human freedom does not diminish the power of God's grace to work miracles in the world and in our hearts. But pondering her experiences of loss in light of a much deeper appreciation of the mysterious event of the Annunciation gave Sally new insights on faith. Faith is always a risk. When we say yes to God, we do not know what challenges we might face.

Sally then reflected again on her own choice to be open to conceiving another child. "There was a specific moment in between my second and third miscarriage when I made a decision to be open to another pregnancy and said 'yes' to God. Even if my pregnancy didn't end well, I told my husband something mystical and spiritual was happening that I couldn't explain. But I had to trust God and see if I could bear a child."

Saved by Hope

To help Sally understand why I was so certain she would rejoice when she is reunited with her children, I shared with her more of my personal story that she had read about in the article I wrote about my pilgrimage to Fátima. In that article, I reflected on my grief after the death of a student I mentored named John who died of cancer when he was twenty-six. In my eulogy to John that I delivered at St. Patrick's Cathedral in New York City in 2019, I reassured John's grieving loved ones that we shall see John again. Together we shall rejoice with John in the presence of our creator.

Despite having spoken those words, I often found it hard to hold on to hope. At times, I felt no spiritual consolation—just darkness.

I shared with Sally that I had promised John that if he survived, we would go on a Marian pilgrimage together. I decided to keep that promise, believing John would be with me on my pilgrimage, albeit in a different way.

When I arrived in Fátima about six months after John's death, I felt empty inside. I was in excruciating pain in my knee from having been hit by a car while walking across the street in Princeton. Nonetheless, I gave my body and my will over to the many rituals around me, which helped me to connect to a reality beyond immediate appearances: kneeling and praying in penance, attending Mass, Eucharistic adoration, and praying the rosary. I meditated on Jesus's march to Calvary while walking around the Stations of the Cross, a visual depiction of fourteen Scriptural passages related to the passion of Christ.

Christian rituals are so powerful precisely because they open our hearts to a deeper reality that is present already. When a loved one dies, our hearts long for the future reunion to become real in the here and now. Christian hope is not the same as progress, which is understood as overcoming dependency and achieving ever-greater autonomy by using reason, strategic rationality, and manipulating things with technology and science. Christian hope is grounded in faith that we are creatures of God.

Prior to going to Fátima, I read *Spe Salvi* ("Saved by Hope"), a 2007 pastoral letter written by Pope Benedict XVI.[4] He writes that Christian hope is not a promise that we will avoid suffering or triumph over evil; Christian hope stems from our relationship with a personal God who promises to walk with us through the valley of death (Psalm 23:4). The death of a young person like John, and the loss of babies in the womb that Sally experienced three times, call out for the language of hope grounded in faith, transcendence, presence, awareness, and love—not a utopian optimism built on the shaky ground of our modern illusions of progress, control, and efficiency.

At times, my prayers seem to go unanswered, and I am sorrowful. But the answer to my prayers is already there in my heart, if I can slow down, listen, and become aware of God's presence. Even when confronting darkness, my faith gives me hope in eternal life, and with that hope I can always grow in love. As Benedict wrote, "faith draws the future into the present, so that it is no longer simply a 'not yet.' The fact that this future exists changes the present; the present is touched by the future reality." During my trip to Fátima, I felt keenly the pain of John's loss and his presence with me, pulling me towards the future reality of our eternal life.

In *Spe Salvi*, Benedict XVI raises the question that Sally and I each faced: Why do we have hope at all? Having traveled to a holy place, the "why" I should live and struggle to have hope seemed to be exactly what I was doing in Fátima because I encountered a "who": a loving God, whom I can serve and praise in this life and who consoles me in my sorrow. As Benedict XVI explains:

> God is the foundation of hope; not any god, but the God who has a human face and who has loved us to the end, each one of us and humanity in its entirety . . . his Kingdom is present whenever he is loved and wherever his love reaches us. His love alone gives us the possibility of soberly persevering day by day, without ceasing to be spurred on by hope, in a world which by its very nature is imperfect.[5]

Contemplating these words brought back to my heart the hope I had expressed during John's eulogy. Our pain when a loved one dies is a sign that we all participate in a love that is greater than all of our suffering. It is that love I went to Fátima searching for; it is that love that came to me through Mary's embrace at Fátima and that came to Sally in her visions of Mary. Mary teaches us the meaning of Christian hope: she has walked the path of faith before us, and she holds us, consoles us, and binds us to her son, giving us hope to keep walking towards the restored paradise, the eternal present that at times pierces through our awareness, exposing a tear in the world, a tear which reveals the unity of past, present and future.

Giving In to the Mystery

The more Sally learned about Mary's freedom at the Annunciation and her suffering and compassion at the crucifixion, the more she could slowly "give into the mystery that much of my experience was gracious and beautiful and bewildering in an astonishing way." Yet, at the same time, "much of it was devastating and horrible and painful." As Sally learned, "You can't only make sense of one half."

"Opening myself up to life again did not just happen biologically. I felt like I had died spiritually. But I've made peace with the reality that life will hurt sometimes, and I grew in the knowledge that God breathes life into dead things."

Sally always struggled with the idea that suffering can sanctify us or make us better. But she had to admit that her painful story had profoundly transformed her in ways that made her capable of greater love. "Even when I didn't know if I'd ever have a living child, my pain could be meaningful, could be fruitful. I could maybe love others better or minister to others better."

Sally grappled with anger and resentment inside her. She didn't want her experiences to keep her from being loving to others. "My suffering has made me better in the sense that it has made me a kinder person. I'm less afraid now to sit with someone in their grief and really look into the abyss."

What she had read in the Gospels about Jesus's compassion now also seemed real to her. She grew to see that "God painted scripture to show us that the individual suffering of those women mattered to Jesus, just as ours does." Learning about Mary helped Sally to see differently how Jesus relates to women in Scripture. "My deeper understanding of Mary's story helped me notice how often Jesus meets women where they are in their places of suffering. It would have been very unusual in his times for a man to single out the woman at the well for a conversation, or to allow himself to be touched by a woman who had been bleeding for years."

Given her painful experience, Sally's knowledge of Scripture took on a deeper emotional resonance. "Those things I sort of knew intellectually, but they now strike me on a deep emotional level as revealing God's love."

About a year after I first spoke to Sally, she cautiously yet joyfully shared the news that she was five months pregnant. She had made it past the first trimester of her pregnancy, but she still grappled with fears of yet another lost pregnancy. Pondering Mary's motherhood of Jesus, Sally knew that even if her baby survived the first nine months inside her womb, there was no guarantee that motherhood would not be painful. "The fact that Mary was a mother who knew suffering and grief made me feel less alone. I survived and am still here because of Mary's protection. I know Mary intercedes for me."

As she waited for her baby's birth, Sally decorated the nursery with pictures of Jesus and Mary. One day, I received the joyful news—with pictures—of Sally's baby girl.

"I'm still pondering what my experiences with Mary mean," Sally told me. "But one of the few people I shared those experiences with is a friend who was raised Catholic but then questioned everything and stopped practicing his faith. I was moved when he replied that he was so overjoyed that he said a Hail Mary!"

Over subsequent conversations, as Sally's baby grew and she decided her next steps, Sally discerned more clearly how her experiences with motherhood were both a cross and a gift. She followed a calling to enter into ministry with women who had lost babies, grieving with them, hoping against hope for new life to come into the world, all while knowing Mother Mary holds our children who have gone before us in her bosom until we are all reunited.

"I think Mary is a bridge," Sally said, "and the reason that that is true is because she is human. She's not God. But, in a way, hearing somebody else's human experience can give us hope and faith. It's meaningful when I show up to be with women who have suffered loss and I'm just there, present. They know I've been through what they are going through. To love others is to be there with them even if I can't take away their suffering. My love for them can help them recover faith and hope in God, as Mary's love did for me."

Chapter 5

Signs of Human Dignity

Aidan Hart and Sacred Art

The Great Human Calling[1]

One Friday afternoon in April 2023, master iconographer Aidan Hart beamed with joy as he stood in the living room of my house in Princeton surrounded by nearly one hundred guests. My husband, David, who is one of Aidan's former students, explained how in our home, we created an icon corner to aid us in personal prayer. Small groups then followed David into his home art studio, where he showed them the materials he uses to paint icons: crushed natural minerals in various colors mixed with egg yolk and an array of brushes. David learned from Aidan not just the skills of making art, but that people of all ages and backgrounds can find a personal, meaningful relationship with God by integrating sacred art into their personal and communal prayer.

The guests that day had come to Princeton for a public conference on art, the sacred, and the common good, at which Aidan was to be the keynote speaker. Looking at the guests crowded into every corner of the first floor of my house, I realized what a broad level of interest there is in Aidan's work. Younger and older people, people of Protestant, Catholic,

Orthodox, and no particular faith, had all gathered first to be immersed in how icons are made and then to hear a lecture about why we make sacred art and venerate the people in them.

Decades earlier, Aidan's zeal to bring people to Christ through iconography had deeply transformed my husband's life. Unlike Aidan, who was not raised in a religious family but embraced faith as a teenager, David had been raised Methodist in England and then rejected faith as a teenager before pursuing studies in science and engineering at St. Edmund Hall, Oxford University. It would not be until his late twenties when, facing a void of meaning in his life, David opened his heart to God again. David began to question his atheism and once again considered if Christianity might speak to his heart. David felt called back to God through the beauty of the sacred art and music at the Brompton Oratory, a magnificent Catholic Church in London. Through becoming Catholic and learning iconography from Aidan, David formed a new image of himself as a child of God and discovered a new vocation—to be a sacred artist like Aidan.

Aidan's desire to know, live, and spread the Gospel in both words and images was evident as he enthusiastically lectured to a packed conference hall the following morning. He challenged the audience with poignant questions:

> Do I view other people as my competitors? As my enemies? Do I see them merely as a means of my individual happiness? Do I consider them merely as members of a crowd of humanity, nameless numbers among millions? Or do I see all others as living icons of God,

> potential saints, amazing and unique beings, small gods, sons and daughters of the Most High?[2]

Drawing on the teachings of Irenaeus of Lyon, in the paper he wrote and delivered for the conference, Aidan insisted on the universality of human dignity, saying, "Every person is born a prince or princess, and if they progress in virtues, they will eventually reach their coronation and be anointed as gods by adoption. They will become kings and queens, co-heirs with Christ to rule under the Holy Spirit."[3]

However, he observed that we live in an era marked by a crude materialism that denies human dignity and the goodness of creation. "Ingratitude increases the spiritual hunger of the consumer, and steals food from the hungry," Aidan remarked. "Consumerism does not satisfy. . . . As a liturgical artist, then, in a small way, I participate in the priestly, prophetical, and royal role incumbent on us all—that is, to fashion creation into an even more articulate hymn of praise to God and to offer it back in thanksgiving."[4]

Less than a year earlier, in August 2022, I had first met Aidan at his art studio in Shropshire, England. Following twelve years as a monk, some of which were in Mount Athos and some as a hermit in England, Aidan had discerned he wanted to return to being a layperson who serves the church through his passion of making art.

Over the last few decades, Aidan has gained prominence in the world of sacred art—art created for worship that inspires a sense of divine presence—through the thousands of icons, paintings, frescoes, mosaics, stone and wood carvings, and church furnishings he has created that adorn

Protestant, Catholic, and Orthodox churches in more than twenty-five countries. He was commissioned by King Charles III of Great Britain to paint frescoes for the king's private chapel and to design the anointing screen used in his 2023 coronation. Currently, Aidan teaches sacred art to people of all backgrounds—religious and non-religious—at the King's Foundation School of Traditional Arts in London.

Aidan has not only created thousands of beautiful works of liturgical art, but through his writing and lectures, he advocates for liturgical art's potential to refute a heretical dualism between the material and the spiritual. Aidan powerfully describes how liturgical art reminds us that we are embodied spirits. Humans are a unity of body and soul, and we are destined to participate in divine love. Thus, by helping us experience God through our unified material and spiritual nature, liturgical art combats the heresy that reduces the human person to merely "a body with a brain," while simultaneously addressing another grave heresy: the belief that "we are spirits, and the body is just a discardable shell."

As I glanced at the tools in his workshop and perused the theology books on his shelves, Aidan explained that the modern world is so secular that many people are closed off to the very idea of God. Although when he first encountered the Bible as a teenager he was enthralled by it, he has met many people who lack the zeal for Scripture or a relationship with God that he has. Aidan is persuaded that, even for people who may be closed off to God, as my husband David once was, the beauty people perceive in sacred art can help them discover meaning and lead them to God. He explained that the word "art" comes from the Proto-Indo-European root *ar*, meaning to join things appropriately together. The role of sacred art is thus "to connect us to other people, to the invisible realities of the world, and ultimately, to heaven and God."

Is That in Scripture?

But how did Aidan go from growing up in a non-religious household in New Zealand to becoming a world-renowned iconographer? When I asked Aidan how he became interested in making sacred art, he quickly described a journey of faith that began in his teenage years when he discovered Scripture.

As a teenager in New Zealand, Aidan began reading the Bible on his own. The words of Scripture pierced his heart with a tremendous desire to dedicate his whole life to Christ. Aidan longed to do something great for Christ, so he began fasting as a spiritual discipline. Noticing Aidan's weight loss, one of his high school teachers asked him how he was doing. Aidan shared his newfound love for the Bible. Aidan's teacher, who was a member of a Baptist church, invited him to church, where Aidan found a community that helped him study the Bible even more intensely. Aidan zealously memorized as much of the Bible as he could.

As he discerned God's vocation for him, Aidan longed to integrate all his faculties—his heart, his intellect, his body, and his love of making art—with his faith. Aidan pursued a university education in English literature, mathematics, and biology, training to become a high school teacher.

The first time Aidan experienced a worship service that engaged all his senses—smelling, hearing, seeing, tasting, and touching—was when he began attending an Anglican church in New Zealand. His love for Scripture came alive in this rich tradition of bodily practices and communal worship grounded in the Bible.

Having been raised in an artistic family, Aidan was drawn to a career in art and slowly discovered that his love for art had a place in the church. After a brief period of teaching, he set out to pursue a full-time vocation as a sculptor. When making a sculpture of a human figure, for instance, Aidan's faith helped him see that the person whose image he was shaping in clay was made in God's image and had a profound inner life. But, as an aspiring artist, Aidan was searching for a mentor, a guide, a way to make art "that would convey the spiritual nature of the human person."

Knowing Aidan's quest, a friend suggested that he meet two Orthodox monks, one of whom painted icons. In the Orthodox tradition, Aidan learned that word and image need one another, as "there are some things that images can express that words can't, as well as vice versa." He began to study Orthodox theology through which, drawing on Scripture, Scriptural commentaries, sermons, and hymns of early church fathers, he learned how sacred images both convey literal events from Scripture yet also employ many symbols which help us contemplate the mysteries of the faith.

In Orthodox Christianity, Aidan found a reverence for Scripture that resonated with his teenage quest to memorize and ponder God's word. He also encountered a rich visual tradition of images of Christ, Mary, and the saints, all of which helped him deepen his love for God and strengthen his conviction that every person bears the image of God. Aidan was fascinated to learn how, through iconography, spiritual truths revealed in Scripture can be communicated through material objects. In Orthodox Christianity, he found an integration of the material and the spiritual that enabled him to deepen his personal vocation to create art that ennobles the human person. In his twenties, Aidan joined the Greek Orthodox Church and returned to his birthplace, England. He spent three years of intense mentorship in a local Orthodox church in England, followed by a year in Thessaloniki to study modern Greek. He explored a monastic calling first in Wales, and later as a hermit in Shropshire, England, eventually discerning to follow a vocation to life as an artist, married man, and father.

The Holy Mountain

During the twelve years he spent as a novice monk and before becoming a hermit, Aidan was sent by his archbishop to spend two years at one of the monasteries on the famous Greek peninsula known as Mount Athos. Referred to as the "Holy Mountain," this peninsula in northeastern Greece shoots out thirty miles in the Aegean Sea. The oldest monastery on Mount Athos, called Great Lavra, was founded in 963 AD. Today, twenty monasteries are located in Mount Athos, which is home to around two thousand monks from not only Greece but also Serbia, Romania, Georgia, Russia, and other countries. The natural beauty of the peninsula with forests of oak, pine, and chestnut trees as well as olive groves and vegetable gardens deepened Aidan's love for all created beauty. The monastic life that centers on love for Scripture, strict disciplines of time and fasting, embodied liturgy, and making art that depicts Scriptural events and expresses God's mysterious actions in the world provided numerous practices through which Aidan deepened his faith in Christ and love of Mary.

Since 1046, women have not been permitted on Mount Athos, not even as visitors or pilgrims. Nonetheless, the reverence for the Mother of God is so profound on Mount Athos that an alternative name for this holy place is "The Garden of the Mother of God." Aidan described Mary's motherhood of Christ as a model for the total union with Christ they seek. The desire, the longing, for a total gift of oneself to Christ sustains them during long vigils. Being totally immersed in the Word of God, experiencing union with Jesus like Mary did when he was incarnate in her womb, is the aim of the various liturgical practices at Mount Athos.

He spoke of his calling to an intense life of prayer through the language of synergies. "In Christ is a synergy of our human nature and his divine nature," he explained. Despite the self-sacrifice required in monastic life, "our relationship with God is a synergy where we don't lose our personality, we're not melted into divinity. There is the person of the *Logos*, and we have our own human personhood. The faith is like a love relationship. You don't marry a force and energy. You marry a person."

"Monks, like all Christians," Aidan explained, "seek union with Christ, the bridegroom. This is why there are many vigil services throughout the monastic year, some lasting twelve hours. They demand a great deal of endurance."

Such vigils take place during the night and early morning, typically beginning in the evening and concluding with the Divine Liturgy at dawn. Following the liturgical books that outline various services for different times of day and night, the monks generally stand while they chant hymns, psalms, and prayers for protection from evil spirits, as well as prayers of intercession, and for forgiveness. Readings from the lives of saints or writings of the church fathers offer a break from chanting. Vigils usually conclude with a Eucharistic service at dawn.

As Aidan learned through the Orthodox tradition, material objects made for worship in the church, like sacred art and liturgical hymns, form our hearts to be responsive to God's calls. We learn to read the signs by honing our spiritual intuition and using our freedom to respond to the calls we discern, as Mary did. Aidan insisted in his lecture in Princeton that liturgical art shapes the vision of the world we carry forth beyond the church walls. "Without vision, the people perish, as the prophet warns,"[5] he said, referring to Proverbs 29:18. He firmly believes that "we act as we see, and I believe, worship and its art can profoundly affect how we see ourselves and all creation."[6]

The daily life of a monk focuses on communal and private prayer, asceticism, and work, and within the context of natural beauty, beautiful architecture, Bible manuscripts, liturgical texts, icons, and frescoes that saturate the monasteries with the tangible yet mysterious presence of God. Living within this environment where every carved beam and painted wall served the liturgy, Aidan discovered that art's highest purpose is not self-expression but theophany—the manifestation of God's glory through our co-creation of material beauty.

Surrounded by centuries of artistic traditions and liturgical celebrations dedicated to honoring the Mother of God,

Aidan deepened his knowledge of Mary. For example, during Lent, the liturgical season which prepares for the passion of Christ and his resurrection at Easter, monks chant the Akathist hymn, composed by St. Romanos the Melodist in the sixth century. The hymn repeats many times the Archangel Gabriel's salutation to Mary, "Rejoice," as it moves through various events in salvation history—including Mary's "yes" to the angel at the Annunciation.

Aidan explained how Mary's obedience at the Annunciation was not passive but arose from her careful discernment. "It's easy to think of obedience as something that restricts us—I can't do this or that. But what if we thought of obedience as close listening to God? Then obedience becomes listening more and more to the Word of God, which deepens our union with God."

Through Mary's humble obedience at the Incarnation, she opened the gates of paradise, which we can taste now through an intimate encounter with God. "Through Mary, the whole of human nature's humanity was given to the Logos, the second person of the Trinity."

"Even though the Annunciation happened 2000 years ago in historical time," Aidan said, "I like to think of the events of Christ's life and the life of the Mother of God as a spring. It sprung up 2000 years ago, but that water doesn't just go back into thc ground. It flows forward through time."

Allegorical Titles for Mary

Not only has Aidan painted icons of events from the New Testament where we would expect to see Mary, such as the

Annunciation and the Nativity, but he has also engaged with the tradition of images that depict her as a throne and a gatekeeper. In *Mary Through the Centuries*, Church historian Jaroslav Pelikan has written about how many Christian communities have moved away from the allegorical and figurative reading of Scripture that was common in the early church and medieval Christianity prior to the Reformation and the Enlightenment.

Iconographic imagery, such as that which Aidan makes, continues the allegorical method of reading Scripture that began in early church. In reading the Scriptures themselves, we learn that God does not only communicate with us only in words, but also through signs. However, in many segments of Christian biblical scholarship and devotional life, the loss of allegorical images and titles for Mary has led to what Pelikan describes as an "impoverishment in the attitude towards Mary."[7]

The allegorical approach to Scripture in the early church and medieval era led to a vast array of titles and images of Mary drawing on the Old Testament wisdom literature, such as Woman of Valor. For example, Pelikan writes, "in keeping with the appropriation of Old Testament language in the interest of amplifying the New Testament, she [Mary] came to be seen as the divinely given answer to the question of the final chapter of the Book of Proverbs . . . 'A Woman of Valor, who will find?' (Proverbs 31:10)."[8]

Aidan referred to many artworks he has made that draw on the allegorical titles of Mary. Learning about these titles and the way they are expressed in iconography drew him into a deeper personal relationship with her. For example, when the abbot at his monastery asked him to create a casing for the famous eleventh-century icon of Mary and Jesus known as the *Portaitissa*, or "Gatekeeper," Aidan was thrilled to have the opportunity to use his artistic skills to honor Mary. "Making this throne for the Mother of God over many months drew me really close to Mary." As part of the liturgical rhythm at the monastery, services are conducted in front of the icon daily. Aidan recalled contemplating her image. "The icon shows her with such a compassionate face," he said with a big smile.

Icons often look strange to modern viewers as they do not resemble photographs or naturalistic portraits. They are painted to remind us that the person depicted now exists in the heavenly realm, and they manifest something of the Holy Spirit dwelling in and shining through the saint. Icons of saints, prophets, and the Mother of God all aim to help us reflect on our life in Christ. The tradition of icon painting developed over time to show "the paradox of revelation and mystery, in a tension between the knowable and acceptance of the unknowable, of light and pregnant darkness . . . the icon's strange use of colors, multiview perspective, and fluid time all serve to waken the viewer to another world and reveal a fuller reality than that which is only material."[9]

The tradition of sacred images as a part of worship is not an idolization of the lifeless material on which icons are painted. On the contrary, sacred icons preserve fire by evoking events from the past so that they may still touch us anew today. In his book *Festal Icons: History and Meaning* (2022), Aidan suggests sacred icons enable a pilgrimage of the soul, stating that "each icon is a landscape, with ever new vistas and mysteries to discover."[10]

Aidan insists that we can know God through the *nous*, a Greek word best described as the eye of the heart. As he remarked to me, "the *nous* is not merely a spirit rattling around inside the body. God created us as a union of spirit and flesh, so that through the eye of the *nous*, we can experience God through the material world."

No matter where we are in our faith, it's challenging to comprehend just how much God loves us. That's why, to see the created order as God intended, Aidan describes the need for a *metanoia*—a conversion and a change of the *nous*. Pondering sacred images thus turns our vision away from ourselves to an encounter with the sacred. We need to turn from ourselves to Christ incarnate. In other words, repentance is a change of vision.

Mary as the Throne of God

Aidan further described how images contained in ancient hymns of the early church speak of Mary as a throne of God because at the Incarnation, the Word took flesh in her body. Mary is celebrated as a garden because "the doors of paradise are opened through the Virgin birth," he explained. For Aidan, referring to Mary as the Throne of God is not merely an act of exalting her; it is an acknowledgment of God's love for humankind. This imagery of Mary as the Throne of God is prefigured in the Old Testament. For example, the throne in Solomon's temple was adorned with imagery suggesting divine presence. Mary fulfills and transcends these archetypes; she is not just a container or resting place for divine power, but a living, active being who is collaborating with God to fulfill his purpose.

Icon of the Nativity. By Aidan Hart, in egg tempera on gessoed wooden panel. *Used with permission of the artist.* https://www.aidanharticons.com.

The many titles given to express Mary's motherhood of God, like Throne of God and Gatekeeper, are meant to help us ponder the profound meaning of the Incarnation. One of Aidan's icons of the Nativity, shown on the previous page, illustrates how allegorical titles of Mary help reveal the meaning of her presence at key moments in the New Testament and guide us to contemplate the great mystery of the birth of Christ.

Aidan insists that he makes icons of the Nativity in order to help us experience this event again for the first time, as if we were present at the birth of Christ. Icons of the Nativity invite us to reflect on the paradox of the Incarnation: the union of opposites—infinite becoming finite.

How does sacred art not only depict an historical event, but symbolize the union of two natures in Christ—the *hypostasis*? How does an artist portray this event both like any other birth that took place in a particular time and place, as recounted in Scripture, while also possessing a unique spiritual significance, unlike any other historical birth?

In his book *Festal Icons*, Aidan reflects on how the Scriptures give us many rich details about the birth of Christ that he has incorporated into his icons. For example, Luke 2:11 tells us about his divine origins: "For to you is born this day in the city of David, a Savior, who is Christ the Lord." Luke 2:14 tells us that they saw a multitude of heavenly hosts praising God and saying: "Glory to God in the highest, and on earth and peace among men with whom he is pleased." Scriptures also tell us that when Christ was born, signs were given to the Magi who searched for the baby.

This image of the Nativity that Aidan painted draws much of its symbolism from traditional icons of the Nativity.

For example, the mountain and the cave symbolize the virgin birth, representing both the divinity and humanity of Christ. The mountain symbolizes Mary, while the cave represents her womb. Our gaze rises to the heavens, yet we also encounter Christ in the cave. The old man in front of Joseph is the prophet Isaiah, reminding Joseph that the virgin birth of Christ fulfills a prophecy concerning his divinity.

Our eyes are naturally drawn to Mary, as she is the largest figure. However, it is not Mary herself who is the most important person in Aidan's icon; it is Christ. Mary's position at the center of this image serves to remind us that her natural motherhood is essential to the union of the two natures—divine and human—in Christ.

The icon also visually represents Mary as the Throne of God—she physically supports and presents Christ to the world, just as a throne elevates a ruler to be seen by his kingdom. Yet, unlike an ordinary throne, Mary is not passive; she actively contemplates the mystery before her. This paradox, that Mary is both nurturing Christ as his mother and worshiping him as her God, invites us to reflect on our own relationship with the divine.

Aidan's image shown earlier in this chapter further emphasizes Christ's humanity by depicting the midwives washing the baby Jesus. He has included an element not mentioned in Scripture, but which is part of the iconographic tradition of the Nativity. The midwives at the bottom right of the image highlight the earthly nature of Christ in all the biological realities of his birth: a newborn baby needs a bath.

The Gospel of Luke tells us that Mary wrapped the baby Jesus in swaddling clothes. This icon depicts the swaddling clothes as a linen shroud and places Christ in a cave in the rock that is a tomb as well as a place of birth. Thus, we contemplate the joyous birth of Christ alongside a foreshadowing of his painful death and burial.

In *Festal Icons*, Aidan describes how the direction each person faces within the icon reveals its central meaning:

> Each "actor" in the divine drama offers worship according to their nature. Some figures face and adore Christ in the manger. Some, like the angels, look up to God the Father in heaven in worship. The Virgin Mary looks down at her Son being washed, wondering at the mystery of God's voluntary abasement. In the form of the star, even the heavens themselves descend towards the Child in acknowledgment that Christ is their creator.[11]

This understanding of Mary as a throne connects the material and spiritual in powerful ways. Her physical body became the dwelling place for divinity, yet this role was not passive; it required her active spiritual participation—her "yes" to God's plan. The throne imagery honors both Mary's physical role at the Incarnation—her womb physically contained God—and her humble obedience, returning all praise for her back to God. Titles for Mary like Throne of God are meant to convey the profound intimacy between Christ and his mother. By contemplating her humble obedience to bear God in the world, we are reminded that a similar intimacy is possible between Christ and us. When we elevate Mary to a position on a throne, we are not making her into a goddess. Rather, we are acknowledging the great mystery that the infinite became finite in her womb. Just as Mary shared an intimate bond with her son while remaining herself fully human, we are transformed through grace to partake of the divine life of the Trinity.

Running Away with the Gift

To illustrate the modern difficulties in slowing down to hear the Word of God and perceive our dignity as children of God, when he once lectured to my class about devotion to Mary, Aidan shared a childhood anecdote. He recalled his eighth birthday party when he saw one of his friends walking up the path to his house with a gift. Unable to wait to receive the gift, he ran outside and snatched it from his friend's hands. Aidan then dashed back inside, tore off the wrapping paper, and opened his gift.

Horrified, his mother pulled him aside and reprimanded him for his selfishness.

Reflecting on this event decades later, Aidan said, "I didn't accept my birthday gift as an expression of love from my friend. I just grabbed it."

Some early church fathers, like Ephraim the Syrian, described Adam and Eve eating from the Tree of Knowledge of Good and Evil in the Garden of Eden as a metaphor for how humans are meant to interact with God's creation. Aidan learned from Ephraim the Syrian's writings that if we receive the created world with thanksgiving, then it becomes for us knowledge of good. But Adam and Eve sinned against God because, as Aidan put it, "If we just grab what God has given to us and turn our back on Him to enjoy it for its own sake, then it becomes for us knowledge of evil."

If we sever our body from our soul, then all of material reality risks becoming objects we can possess, rather than gifts to treasure. Aidan shared that childhood incident many decades later when he lectured in one of my classes as an example of how, when we see God's gift approaching, if we rush ahead, grab it greedily, and hide in a corner, we lose the opportunity to connect in love with the gift-giver. Aidan firmly believes that with the aid of liturgical art, we can encounter God through created material. With a transformed vision of ourselves as a unity of body and soul, our actions will flow from love and thankfulness, not greed.

To receive God's gift as a sign of love and not as something we can possess and exchange, we need to experience an inner change. As Aidan explained, if we don't receive God's gifts as an expression of his love, but instead grab them and run away with them, they become for us knowledge of evil. Contemplating sacred art helps us relate to God through love. Ultimately, contemplating God through sacred art is meant to transform our lives from a logic guided by exclusively self-interested exchanges to a logic of gifts.

Too often, the modern world tries to drown out the *being* mode of life and turns our attention to the *doing* mode. The busy-ness of our days and the machinations of our mind often make it hard to enter the attentive mode of being. Do we make time to walk through a park and marvel at just how many shades of green there are in the trees and bushes? How hard is it to put away our smart phones and let our minds relish the silence?

Contemplation starts with a loving attention to reality. Contemplation allows us to rest in God's presence. Contemplation allows us to enter a silence in which we hear God's word in our hearts. Being present to all of reality—without having to always conceptualize our experience or analyze things scientifically—allows us to encounter God intimately and simply, like a child who wonders at the beauty of each flower and rejoices at every bird in the sky.

The Christian calling is ultimately to live a contemplative life while we go about our ordinary work of manual labor and intellectual endeavors. At times, our tendency to analyze, measure, and manipulate needs to be forgone to return to a childlike, simple state of perceiving reality that opens us up to a sacramental way of living—seeing in visible things the invisible grace of God. We need to set aside time to see with the eye of the heart, the *nous*, the *totality* of things, the unity of being and doing, the unity of body and soul, the unity of God with his people, the unity of the divine and the human in Jesus Christ.

But the Christian search for the sacred is never a flight from the world. Christian faith is about letting the Word of God sanctify the world.

Wounded by Beauty

Aidan's caution about the materialism in modern culture resonated with me because, although I would not have called myself a mind-body dualist, I often acted as if I was just a body with a brain. For example, in the spring of 2013, as part of a class I taught that reviewed various theories about human happiness, I took a test of character strengths. I was dismayed to find I scored *lowest* on my appreciation of beauty.

While I was busy climbing the academic ladder of success, I was failing in beauty. I dedicated little time to being in nature or experiencing art and music. Listening to my students who were cynical about the future, I realized that developing our analytical capacities while neglecting the human desire for beauty, as I had done, would not make me or my students happy.

How had I lost my love of beauty? My art history classes during undergraduate studies at Yale University primarily emphasized the brilliance of the artists, favoring abstract expressionism over recognizable forms and celebrating post-modern art trends that seek to unsettle viewers and challenge tradition. Additionally, in my training in psychology and sociology—fields intended to study the human experience and culture—beauty was either completely overlooked as irrelevant to human existence, seen merely as another form of self-promotion, or analyzed as another method through which humans can assert dominance over others.

In the fall of 2013, I moved back to my alma mater of Yale University, where I lived in a faculty apartment located in a student residence. Getting to know students in their everyday lives, I saw how many of them lacked meaning and purpose. The more I read about beauty as part of human happiness, the more I learned that we do not encounter the world either through beauty *or* reason; through intellect *or* intuition. We experience the world as filled with both mystery *and* order. We grasp the meaning of things intuitively *and* possess the intellectual capacity to reflect, discern our callings, and make practical judgments that align with that discernment. Our need for beauty and our rationality are *both* fundamental to being human. But the students I knew were starving for beauty. Too many of them lived on a junk food diet of superficial entertainment.

My search for beauty also led me to appreciate in ways I had not before the beauty of embodied forms of sacred worship with art and music. I tried to stand, watch, and listen to great Christian traditions of embodied liturgies and learn about artistic traditions such as iconography. Even if the experiences can feel a bit strange, just as an icon might look strange the first time you encounter one, by imitating the great traditions that have been handed down for millennia, I have glimpsed a bit better the meaning of the resurrection, and my vision has been opened to await with greater desire the second coming of Christ.

When I met my husband, David, in 2022 at the age of forty-seven, we discovered we were both on a path where the search for the beautiful was leading us to God. I had founded a nonprofit, The Scala Foundation, around six years earlier to transform culture through beauty, creativity, and joy. David is a talented visual artist and longs to teach about great traditions of sacred art to young artists and anyone, like me, who appreciates art even if I don't make it. The cultivation and appreciation of the beautiful created a common ground for our relationship to flourish. I shared my love of literature and poetry, and he taught me more about his art. We both love music and the beauty of nature. In our marriage, our everyday life is enriched in countless ways by our passion for beauty. Our work together allows us to share our enthusiasm for beauty with others more powerfully with our complimentary talents.

Although speaking of the importance of beauty now comes naturally to me, it is harder for me to find time to create beauty. With David, I sing in a church choir. I started taking voice lessons, which I thoroughly enjoy. But I never thought I would learn to paint icons—it seemed beyond my reach.

But, in the summer of 2025, along with David, I attended a ten-day iconography workshop in Crete led by master iconographer George Kordis. Although George endlessly encouraged me, my attempts to imitate his beautiful drawing style seemed to me quite pathetic. I've never been talented at drawing. While the other beginner and advanced learners flew past me with their skills, I sat alone in a corner. I struggled to even draw the outline of a face or an eye. Once again, I was failing at beauty.

Then an art teacher from Macedonia approached me. Surveying my attempts to make an icon, she assured me that even a series of lines done well would suffice for a day's effort. She kindly helped me draw a whole page of just the shape of the face one day, then just the eyes one day, and then just noses the next day. My grumbling and resistance—grounded in my pride—slowly melted as I humbled myself to follow a master, even if all I could do was repeat the same baby steps. After a week of intense instruction, in the contours of the head, the eyes, the nose, there eventually emerged a drawing of the face of a saint in the iconographic style. As basic as my drawings were, I realized that the difficulties I had in depicting the human face made me appreciate the dignity of the human person. We are made in the image of God, a truth conveyed by each and every human face.

Drawing the human face in the iconographic style, albeit through repeated baby steps, deepened my love for liturgy that venerates the people depicted in icons. While staying at the Orthodox Academy of Crete for that workshop, we attended several liturgies at the Holy Monastery of Gonia. When I walked into the Sunday liturgy by myself, I hesitated. I wasn't sure how to engage. All around me were icons and candles. Several monks chanted in Greek in front of the iconostasis—a series of icons behind which lay the tabernacle and the altar.

Even though I do not speak Greek, I tried to unite my prayers to the liturgy around me by meditating on my morning prayers in front of a crucified Jesus, repeating Psalm 51:1–3: "Have mercy upon me, O God, according to the steadfast love; according to thy abundant mercy blot out my transgression. Wash me thoroughly from my iniquity and cleanse me from my sin! For I know my transgressions and my sin is ever before me."

I observed others around me, looking for clues as to what else I could do to join in these prayers. When a father picked up his son, who kissed an icon of the Mother of God holding Jesus at the entrance of the church, I asked myself: Is that just a mindless action that is part of a meaningless ritual? Or it is a symbol of reverence for a living tradition that carries forth a mystery—that we await the *Parousia*, the second coming of Christ?

Peering over the shoulder of that father, I realized that his actions—and mine—demonstrate how tradition works: we imitate, observe, integrate, search, and let our desire for

God increase as we discover new ways to immerse ourselves in God's word.

I followed the father closer to where the monks were chanting. I did my best to imitate and therefore participate in the long liturgy. During the hour and a half of standing, bowing, kneeling, and crossing myself, I made a mental note of the few Greek words I understood from the liturgical chants and prayers.

Just as somehow, I put together small pieces of the iconography lesson into the basic contours of the human face, I realized that when I listened closely to what the monks where chanting, and to the priest's homily, the few words I understood formed a rich tapestry of meaning.

During the chanted liturgy, some of those words I understood included *hagios*, which means "holy," and was most often repeated three times, as in the Book of Revelation 4:8. *Hagios. Hagios. Hagios.* Holy. Holy. Holy. I also recognized the words Cherubim and Seraphim. The prayers spoke of *Theo* (God) and *Theotokos* Maria (Mary, the God Bearer). I recognized *Christos* and *Kyrie Eleison*—which are words in the Roman Catholic liturgy we often say in Greek—appealing to the Lord for his mercy. When I heard words that sounded like the English words "One," "Holy," "Catholic," and "Apostolic Church," it dawned on me that the words I recite weekly in the English version of the Nicene Creed came from Greek.

During the priest's homily, would I be able to capture enough words to know what he was talking about? To my amazement, with just five words that I understood—*Parousia* (second coming), *Mysterion* (mystery), *Metamorphosis* (transfiguration), *Prosopon* (Face of a Person), and *Agape*

(Self-Giving Love), I stitched together just once sentence I could deeply contemplate: we rejoice in contemplating the mystery that, through Christ, we are transformed from sinners to persons capable of receiving God's pure gift of love.

A few days later, when I returned to the monastery to participate in some of its twelve-hour vigil and Eucharistic service in honor of the feast of the Dormition of the Mother of God celebrated every year on August 15, a feast to which thousands of pilgrims flocked, I recognized the same sound of the chant to the Akathist hymn, which repeats "Rejoice." Celebrating Mary's Dormition as we did at the Gonia Monastery reminded us that as Mary is enjoying the fruits of the resurrection, we can all journey together towards the *Parousia*—our new life. During the chanted prayers, I gazed at icons of the Transfiguration of Christ (*Metamorphosis* in Greek) and of Mary's Dormition.

The sacred images of the Mother of God that permeated the liturgical space encouraged reverence for her. At the end of the liturgy, I watched as a mother picked up her daughter, who kissed an icon of Mary's Dormition. I glanced up at Jesus on the cross with the two thieves to his right and left, and I asked for the grace to be a repentant sinner who believes in God's mercy and in our great calling to bear God's image in the world, as Mary did.

The icons David and I made at the workshop in Crete, the icons we venerate at home, the icons Aidan makes for churches all around the world, the ancient icons we saw all around Crete in monasteries that are over a thousand years old, all bring the eternal present to us and lead us on a path of divinization—a path through Calvary and repentance, but always a path of hope and light, of communion with each other and the Trinity.

Peering into the great mysteries of the faith and humbling myself to learn the craft of iconography from a master required a childlike openness. What kept me from pursuing my love of beauty too often was my pride in my intellect; what often kept me from imitating Mary's humility has been my attachment to one or another form of power.

Aidan helped me, David, and countless others who have read his books, heard his lectures, seen his art, or taken his iconography classes to understand that the great tradition of sacred art helps us to venerate Mary. We venerate Mary so that we may imitate her, and in imitating her, we may be ever more transformed into the image of God and see the great dignity in every human face.

Getting to know Mary has opened for Aidan the meaning of the many prophecies in the Scriptures. Mary's words in the Gospel may be few, but depicting Mary as the Throne of God reminds us that sacred images can be what Aidan called physical prophecies, objects that communicate the meaning of the Incarnation that happened. During one conversation about the Annunciation, Aidan remarked that this feast is also "very Pentecostal." He asked rhetorically, "Do you want the Holy Spirit to dwell in you? Although Mary is greater than all human beings created on this earth, the Annunciation is not just about the dignity of just one person. What happened at that moment, the coming of the Holy Spirit into Mary, could happen to us all. At every liturgy, the priest calls down the Holy Spirit, not just on the gifts of bread and wine, but also upon us. So every liturgy is an annunciation."

Chapter 6

Echoes of the Annunciation

James MacMillan and Mary's Creative Inspiration

From Scottish Coal Country to Composing Music for Her Majesty's Funeral

Sir James MacMillan's musical compositions, widely recognized by secular and religious audiences alike, have been called ecstatic and a deep spiritual journey. Queen Elizabeth II awarded him knighthood in 2015 for his outstanding contributions to the world of music, including his orchestral works, operas, concertos, and sacred choral music. Several years later, for the queen's funeral, he composed a piece titled "What Shall Separate Us?," one of his many musical meditations on suffering and redemption. But for decades, as he rose to prominence in the largely secular world of classical music, James kept up his guard and rarely spoke of his Christian faith.

I first met James in person in Princeton in 2023 during a summer program where he was teaching young composers and choral conductors. I had read a series of his essays, including a reflection on composing music to express the profound human suffering Mary experienced at the passion of Christ. When we sat down to talk about how his faith influences his work in music and how he strives to bring the love of music back to concert halls, churches, and to the elderly and disabled through the Cumnock Tryst music festival in Scotland, I was intrigued by his humility, his soft Scottish accent, and his deep insights on Mary as a source of inspiration for creative artists. Drawing on his understandings of Christian contemplative prayer, I marveled at how different he was from the stereotype of a suffering artist who expresses the misery we all supposedly feel about the human condition. Despite his ability to provoke rapturous applause worldwide with his compositions and conducting, he did not conform to the image of the artist as a demi-god who, through his own creative powers, leads others to unparalleled spiritual heights.

Over time, James has grown more certain that the Holy Spirit somehow mysteriously guides his creative intuition. During one interview when he was asked about where he found inspiration, James somewhat unguardedly replied that he believed in divine inspiration. He initially regretted that spontaneous utterance, feeling vulnerable and exposed as a person of faith, awaiting what he had previously experienced when making similar comments: an inevitable avalanche of mockery. But instead of a sarcastic "huh?" or "ha!" or "c'mon!" the interviewer was intrigued, even calling his response "non-conformist" and "avant-garde."[1]

That moment marked for James a rather seismic shift in his world of music, marking an openness to deeply theological reflections on music. In numerous ways, such as by composing music that invites us to meditate on the mystery of suffering and redemption, speaking of musical analogies like the fugue, and maturing in faith through facing the abyss of loss, James turned to Mary for inspiration. If, for many secular lovers of music, music is a window that may open them to the divine, for James, Mary is likewise a window that opens his heart to the divine.

The Passion, the Abyss, and the Light[2]

In 1959, James was born in Kilwinning in the southwest of Scotland to a Catholic family of coal miners in the county of Ayrshire, in what seems like an unlikely beginning for one of the most celebrated music composers and conductors alive today. James remembers that he first wanted to compose music at the age of ten. With the demise of the coal industry that had employed his grandparents and many other family members, there was no clear vocational path for a young man like James. But while he grew up in poverty, the practice of music at home, especially Scottish brass band instrumental music, was embedded in his daily life. As a young lad at Catholic Mass, hymns like the Stabat Mater, a meditation on Mary's suffering at the foot of the cross, moved James's heart. Music was also part of the school curriculum. His love for music, and his romance with a young woman named Lynne, who would later become his wife, kept him very engaged with his high school choir.

James longed to follow the call to a life of music, but there was no set path for him to take. He kept learning as much as he could about folk, rock, classical, and sacred music. With his "idealistic and ideological nature," he also felt a deep longing to do something about social issues.[3] As he ventured out of Scotland and met composers who also cared about humanitarian issues, he found their approach often "romantically revolutionary" but lacking in practical engagement with the world.[4] His personal quest—how his love for music and his ideals might reinforce each other—seemed at first to be a stumbling block. But slowly, he discovered more of his Catholic tradition about the nature of our calling to holiness that emphasizes divine-human interaction as part of creativity.

James wrestled with what felt like a "schizophrenic existence," a seemingly unbridgeable gap between his faith and his music. His deepest desires for faith and justice felt compartmentalized from each other. "Catholicism has always meant a lot to me," James wrote, "but in those early days I couldn't see any way of allowing the religious dimension into the practice of my music, and, of course, those who flattered themselves that they were at the cutting edge of this particular art form would say that there was no place for something as reactionary and anachronistic as the Catholic faith in the modern artistic world."[5]

He lamented how "a lot of recent so-called spiritual music can be a mono dimensional experience of transcendence without a sense of sacrifice," as if a musical experience could bypass the deepest abysses of the human condition.[6] But even outside of religious circles, James noticed that the story of Mary's pain at the foot of the cross seemed to speak to a universal desire for hope. As a composer, he wished to avoid any sugar-coating of human suffering. Rather, he turned to Christian narratives that illustrated how the path to the resurrection passes through the cross. Being drawn to what he deemed "the sacrificial aspect of the great Christian narrative,"[7] he began to compose music that he likened to a poetic meditation on the passion of Christ.

In compositions that reflect upon the passion of Christ, James found a way to see the face of God. As Mary knew, we do not come to the light without experiencing the dark. To come into the light, we must ponder *who* it is that can pull us out of that darkness. Why would there be resolution to the darkness and not just a pure abyss of nothingness? Could the encounter with the abyss somehow be the path to see the face of God? As he has written,

> To avoid the darkness and the tragedy is to refuse to face up to the abyss, which is our human experience. It is a flight from reality and from the true nature of God. Spirituality is not just some sort of easily won, feel-good factor. Spirituality is something that you find in the here and now, in the fears, aspirations, joys, and tragedies of human life, in the grit and mire of daily existence, which then raises incredible possibilities of compassion in those encounters.[8]

Does the Bible Command Us to Be Creative?

James shared how secular interviewers often have implied that traditional religious piety, like his Catholic faith, would somehow suppress true creativity. Isn't it true, the argument goes, that true creativity emerges only when we reject any external crutch and forge our own sense of meaning? Isn't turning to tradition for inspiration therefore failing to take responsibility for using our human faculties to the full—to think, create, fashion, move forward?

One way James has responded to this question is by going to the Scriptures for insights on human creativity. Pondering the creation story in Genesis, James noted that the creative impulse seems to be akin to the pathos—the exuberant love—with which God looked upon the world at the dawn of creation. As a musician, James longs to craft something beautiful, to take disparate elements of sound and word and fashion them together. The artistic fecundity he eagerly seeks he also longs to connect to his faith in order to understand what it means for him as a composer to "be open to the will of God; clues to how one can become a channel for the divine will, without diminishing one's own God-given free will."[9]

Whether it be folk music, classical music, or music for the liturgy, James describes the nature of the creative process as akin to fashioning something new out of "embers of an old fire extracted and gathered up and waft it into a new flame."[10]

The Latin word *inspiratio*, James explained, translates to "in-breathing." To be inspired is not simply self-expression emerging; inspiration signifies an infusion from outside us that enters within. Creation is therefore co-creation with God, a fusion of something profound within us and something external capable of stretching, changing, and deepening even our most ingrained instincts.

James described to me how, for a creative artist, being fruitful and creating "means we have the freedom to choose to let the spirit in. Perhaps the artist's response is analogous to Mary's response at the Annunciation."

As he studied the Scriptures, James was drawn to the idea of Mary as a vessel of the Holy Spirit. "Although it is not popular today to talk about obedience," he said, "Mary obeyed

God's will when she said yes at the Annunciation." However, her obedience did not stem from servile fear or mere passivity, but a willingness to be transformed by her encounter with God. "You can't enter into the presence of God in a state of defiance and resistance. You have to surrender some of your ego. You must be open to the possibility of being changed." Mary's freedom was engaged when she said "yes" to the prompting of the Holy Spirit at the Annunciation. She breathed in the spirit and conceived a child in her womb, beginning the redemption of all of creation.

Mary's freedom at the Annunciation was more than a choice or exercise of autonomy. It was a free offering of her entire being, a self-sacrifice to receive the in-pouring of the Holy Spirit and to bring into the world a new creation, Jesus, who united the divine and the human in a truly unique way. Drawing on church fathers and Catholic teachings, James insists that Mary was not commanded by God at the Annunciation. Yet, her freedom at the Annunciation was much more than a simple choice to say yes or no; her freedom meant she was willing to be stretched and changed by her cooperation with God.

It's the interaction between the human and the divine at the Incarnation that enlivens James's faith. He's certain that, if he allows it, he, too, can be a vessel for the Holy Spirit to enter the world through his music. In the act of composing, James engages all his faculties: his intellect, emotions of fear and joy, and his body, his very flesh and blood convulsing from inside him to externalize what is in his head to create something new. As James wrote, "the incarnation came about through Mary's free and rational acceptance of God's plan for her. Similarly, an artist or a composer who thinks in real and meaningful terms of a divine inspiration would be mistaken in underestimating the full and active participation of all one's human faculties."[11]

All Christians, James therefore believes, can look to Mary at the Annunciation and ponder the image of a woman's body becoming receptive to the "seed of God's word" and seek to imitate Mary's example as we wait to be filled, to be unified with God, and bring forth fruit from that union.

James suggested that "there's something about the biblical tradition that almost compels us to be creative." Mary's obedience at the Annunciation is followed quite quickly in Scriptures with her prophetic voice in the Magnificat. Her reply to Elizabeth, who calls her "the mother of my Lord" (Luke 1:43), gives all praise back to God, expressing trust in him that, through what he is doing in her, the world order will be turned upside down. Drawing on her knowledge of the Scriptures, in particular the canticles of Judith and Hannah, Mary composes her own canticle. The paradoxes, the overturning of everything, will uplift the meek and humble, depose the rich and powerful, and "scatter the proud in the imagination of their hearts" (Luke 1:51).

James pointed out that Mary was creative with the Scriptures when composing the Magnificat. She uniquely combined familiar words and images from various parts of Scripture—the canticle of Hannah, the canticle of Judith, and the Psalms. "If you examine Mary's song, the Magnificat," James said, "you realize that all of Mary's words stemmed from the Old Testament Scriptures, which she would have prayed daily."

James described Mary's words in the Magnificat as illustrating how "through the breath of God, Mary is inspired to see a new world. Her eyes are opened to a frighteningly radical overturn of everything that is accepted—an end to tyranny and oppression. . . . Through Mary's example, we learn to see beyond the apparently obvious and predetermined past of human behavior."[12]

Speaking softly, he shared the thought-provoking idea that "perhaps it is not too fanciful to say that every musical composition is a little incarnation." By transforming an instinct or idea into a new musical creation, every new piece of art is what he calls "an echo of the Annunciation . . . it's the taking flesh of something from this interaction between the human person and the divine, between one's artistic vision and skills and a truth in-breathing of something outside us that makes it all come alive."

Thus, like Mary's Magnificat, James believes that "similarly, today's composers and artists draw inspiration from the Bible to create something that is new yet also rooted in tradition."

Out of the Ashes of Loss Comes Inspiration

James's inner life became dark after the loss of his granddaughter Sara Maria, who had been born with severe disabilities, at the tender age of six. In his grief, he could not compose music. He leaned even more on Scriptural accounts of suffering and rebirth through liturgical prayer and personal, contemplative prayer. He searched for, and eventually found, a light in the darkness and began to write music again that expresses both the joys and lament of life.

On the day Sara Maria was born, her mother, James's daughter Catherine, brought a small radio with her to labor and delivery. When she turned it on, the music of BBC Radio 3 filled the air with James's setting of "O Bone Jesu," a meditation on the passion of Christ. Hearing words about God's mercy set to music felt fitting as Sara Maria entered the world, as her brain had not developed properly in the womb. Her birth brought the family great joy, but her health was fragile, and her development was significantly impaired.

James and his wife, Lynne, threw themselves into helping their daughter care for Sara Maria. In between her many hospital visits, they introduced her to their love for music. Despite her many limitations, Sara Maria relished sitting on James's lap and pounding notes on the piano with him.

In the months leading up to her death, he composed a new setting of the Stabat Mater. He could sense a personal loss coming, and news of tragic world events crashed into his consciousness, leading him to search for hope in the cross. His family longed to imitate Mary's presence at the foot of the cross, yearning for Jesus to draw "all human life, and death, towards him."[13]

The fifteenth-century Russian Orthodox iconographer Andrei Rublev created a famous depiction of the Trinity. In this image, the three figures form a circle of contemplation. None of the figures looks directly at the viewer; instead, they engage in an eternal exchange of loving glances with each other. For James, that image of the Trinity allowed him to gaze into what he referred to as the monstrous ocean of God's love. By contemplating the Trinity with the help of an icon, James described how we begin to see not an abyss but the divine presence that envelops us.

Through practicing contemplative prayer, James began to recognize how silence is not absence but presence. When we journey down our road to Calvary, Christ is with us, often in silence. Nonetheless, we can discern a silent presence that accompanies us even in our darkest hours. For James, silence became a means of deepening his knowledge of God, transcending words or sounds.

Over time, Sara Maria's absence was transformed into a presence of a different kind, a memory that is alive, still reaching him. As he reflected, "She fills all our silences—with memories of smiles and delight, love and commitment, loss and pain. I'm sure it has been she, sometimes, who has infused the sounds that well up in my mind and lead to the music I've written since. In the silence, I hear her."[14]

The Fugue and Human Freedom

Musical analogies are often used to describe the ascent of the human soul to God—or better put, God's humble descent to us.

During one of my conversations with James, I mentioned that in Caryll Houselander's book *Reed of God*, a powerful literary meditation on Mary, she speaks of Mary as a fugue, drawing us closer to God. Houselander describes how "the fugue is the music of the Word of God, God's spoken Word, telling His love; and the motif is always gathered back to be concentrated again in its simplicity."[15]

James explained that a fugue is a kind of melody, in which a melodic fragment—usually one voice or instrument referred to as the "subject"—leads the way. Then another voice enters in at a different pitch. As more voices enter, they each respond to the "fugual subject" at a relative pitch. "Eventually, there's a building up of a number of different parts, all based on the same material, all based on the same musical DNA, so that there's an interaction of line and voice which creates a unity. There can be one hand on the keyboard doing one voice, and other hands on the keyboard doing another voice. Maybe the feet on the organ are doing a third voice. It can seem very diverse and separate, but it's absolutely connected in a unity because the musical DNA of the subject, the first thing we hear, permeates the whole thing."

As Houselander puts it, in our winding journey of the spiritual life, we can turn to Mary as our Mother, and with her, we always return to the beginning—to a lyrical simplicity that can purify us. I eagerly shared with James why I love the analogy of Mary as a fugue, wondering if, as a musical expert, he would understand what I meant.

"The idea of a fugue reminds us that God attracts us to Him in love," I said. "Mary heard God's call two thousand years ago and responded with her whole being. We, too, have the freedom to respond to God's calls. We are meant to come to God through the body of Christ, and if we bind ourselves to Mary as our spiritual mother, our weaknesses become less relevant because we are part of a fugue—Mary leads the way. Mary is a subject, a person, who calls each of us. Our response to Mary binds us to her and to others without dissolving our uniqueness. Out of many sequential calls and responses emerges an incredible harmony that expresses a profound unity in difference."

"The analogy of a fugue is fitting because Mary is both

united with God and distinct from him," James replied. "A fugue is contrapuntal. It's the separateness of musical material being embraced and brought together by the composer. All these different components could possibly be chaotic, distinctive, and antagonistic. But a composer brings these different elements together not just to co-exist but to build an unthought-of unity. At the Annunciation, Mary's freedom did not vanish; instead, her unity with God arises from a tension that beautifully intertwines the human and the divine."

The analogy of a fugue is critical to seeing Mary's purity as something much greater than passivity; it is openness to inspiration. Mary's purity is akin to lyrical simplicity—self-sacrifice. Opening ourselves to profound unity with God is the most creative thing we can do because God's word alive in us makes us into who he is calling us to become.

Mary at the First Pentecost

I shared with James how when I was invited to put together a chapel service at Princeton Theological Seminary remembering Mary in Scripture, I included short reflections on her presence at three key moments in the New Testament: the Annunciation, the Crucifixion, and Pentecost. At the service, I combined Scriptures from each of those events with a work of art to contemplate and a song we sang together.

Although Mary's presence at both the birth and death of Christ is commonly recalled, it is less discussed—even among Pentecostal Christians I've spoken to—that she was present at the first Pentecost. We do not know what Mary said or did at Pentecost, as her words are not recorded in Scripture. But we do know she was present there in the upper room. And we know that she was she was always fully receptive to the Holy Spirit.

Mary's name is not explicitly mentioned during the dramatic narrative of Pentecost in Acts 2. But a few verses earlier, in Acts 1:14, Scripture powerfully affirms her presence in the upper room: "All these with one accord devoted themselves to prayer, together with the women and Mary the mother of Jesus, and with his brethren."

After Pentecost, the followers of Christ were emboldened to go forth to teach and to preach. Being filled with the Spirit, then as well as now, manifests as gifts of prophecy and healing. Pentecost is often regarded as the reversal of Babel (Genesis 11:1–9), a time when language was confused and scattered. At Pentecost, everyone understood the Spirit's words in their own languages.

James's insights on the nature of divine inspiration in human creativity led me to make a suggestion at the service that I hoped would inspire people to take up the call to co-create with God in praising Mary through song: what if we considered musical creativity as one of the gifts of the Spirit, like one of God's commissions to the disciples at Pentecost?

"The outpouring of the Holy Spirit at Pentecost inspires us to praise Mary in song," I said. "That is why praises exist in every tongue and in every nation where Christ is followed, songs that lift up prayers for unity among the children of God who have the same mother, songs that invite us to imitate Mary's hope and courage at the crucifixion so that we take up our call at Pentecost," I continued. "When we sing praises of Mary we form a body of worshipers, and that pleases God.

One of the greatest gifts of music to the church is that music unites us—not just in our hearts—but in our bodies, giving worship to God."

If one reason to commemorate Pentecost is because all Christians breathe in the Holy Spirit, are transformed by grace, and are sent out to share the good news using our unique gifts—one of which is artistic creativity—then it seemed fitting to bring art into this worship service at a church with no sacred art. In the worship aide for that service, I included an image of Mary at Pentecost that Jean Restout painted in 1732, which is now hanging in the Louvre Museum in Paris. In this image, the Holy Spirit is depicted as light and fire. The disciples and Mary are together, receiving the gifts of healing, prophecy, and speaking in tongues.

The congregation sang "Veni Sancti Spiritus" (Come, Holy Spirit) over and over again, set to music by the Taizé Community, an ecumenical community founded in France known for their hospitality to people of all Christian denominations and to seekers. My husband, David, researched ancient Byzantine hymns to Mary, and we worked with the worship leaders on how to adapt the language for that audience. The result combined faithfulness to Scripture, poetic imagination from tradition, and our slight adaptations for twentieth-century Christians who are mostly newcomers to praising Mary during a worship service.

While the body of worshipers called repeatedly to the Holy Spirit, David chanted these words slowly, in a voice amplified by the microphone:

Hail, Mary, full of grace, the Lord is with you;

your praise is beyond the eloquence of the most cultured
tongues,
and every mind is amazed at your birth-giving;
henceforth, all ages will call you blessed.
I want to sing of the virginal fountain of Life,
who alone held in her womb the Word
who heals the ills of humankind.
He now sits at the right hand of the Father
and sends down upon us the grace of the Spirit.
We, on whom the breath of God's grace has blown,
have become luminous and bright.
We are changed in a resplendent manner as we
contemplate the
Wisdom of the undivided Trinity, glorifying the triple
Radiance.

Just as beautiful singing can release the divine energy of the Holy Spirit into the world, our love for Mary unites us to the body of Christ, the church. The love for Mary expressed through art and music across time and space serves as a culturally creative force in the world, fostering unity and love.

Perhaps the most powerful moments in Scripture when we are invited to imagine unity in faith is at the Ascension and Pentecost. At both, the church's prayer is sustained by Mary's prayer, united together in hope, as in a fugue. Mary reaches out to each of us, pulling us to her son. Some songs of praise for Mary have been heard for 1,800 years, and some music is new, but it all ties together. Sacred music reaches out, pulls us in, and brings us together. Singing Mary's praises is part of our response of awe and gratitude for God's love that goes back toward God in a cycle of exit and return.

The Vocation of an Artist

Secular interviewers, at least some in the past, tended to view James's faith as a crutch. Isn't it the responsibility of the artist, the argument goes, to simply embrace the void, to refuse to rely on emotional or religious crutches, and forge meaning out of nothing? If the artist's role is to make his own meaning, wouldn't relying on religious texts, sacred stories, and pious practices suppress the total freedom of the artist to be creative? How could a *real* artist fall back on any kind of traditional, and therefore false, sense of meaning?

One way to think of the modern view of the artist is as a demigod, who can be thought of as modern-day Promethean figure. In Ancient Greek myths, Zeus, the king of the gods, sequestered fire among only the gods, keeping it secret from humans. Prometheus was a Titan, a semi-divine figure, who became so enamored with humans that he turned his back on Zeus, the supreme god. Prometheus stole fire from the gods and brought it to humanity, sharing its secret knowledge and power with them.

This Promethean demigod, somebody who can take divine inspiration, possess it, and then bring it into the human realm, represents a false divinization of the human person. If we steal our creative power rather than receive it as a gift, then we assume that God doesn't love us. If we are in competition with God, then in order to get what we long for, we must steal from him our delight, our happiness, and fulfillment. Human creativity thus becomes something we do apart from God.

Picturing Mary at the Annunciation offers a very different model for artists. The angel Gabriel appeared to her, offering a surprising and unprecedented gift from God, and she responded with acceptance and cooperation. Musical analogies for understanding Mary, such as fugue and silence, help us to understand the meaning of the incarnation, which required human cooperation with grace. Our love for Mary expressed in music and art is a culturally creative force, what James called "little incarnations" through which we give all of ourselves, our creativity, back to God in a cycle of exit and return.

Both accounts of divine influences on human creativity—Prometheus and Mary at the Annunciation—share a sense of mysterious divine inspiration at work in the world. But in the Promethean understanding of creativity, the human with inspiration can turn his back on God and do whatever he wants. In contrast, an artist who takes seriously the meaning of what happened at the Annunciation humbly extends that incarnational moment into his art.

Jacques Maritain, one of the twentieth century's most influential philosophers, sought to redress the Promethean view of art with a view of creativity as cooperating with God. Poetry and art emanate from the deepest recesses of our soul, Maritain writes, but are "in no way for the sake of the ego."[16]

In the modern world, Maritain lamented that artists are often seen as heroes who expresses their subjectivity with supreme freedom. Like James, Maritain feared the culturally corrosive idea that art expresses the "quest for the human subject's omnipotence." But that omnipotence is not true freedom, Maritain warned. It is false to assert that in creativity, "the soul believes it is transferred above everything and enjoys infinite liberty."[17]

The Promethean view of the artist isolates his vocation entirely within himself, while at the same time positing that an artist's self-expression can somehow become the basis of a collective conscience for society. An artist may be inspired to create objects, and those new things may, in fact, direct the inspirations of a collective group But only God is the author of the human conscience.

As James well knows, the meaning he sought to create in his music passes through him mysteriously, but he is not the origin of that meaning. Like Mary, James longs for his musical creativity to cooperate with God's redemptive, beautiful work in the world. In contrast, the vocation of an artist understood as egocentric self-expression threatens to become a dark mysticism that misdirects our collective spirit away from a unity of truth, beauty, and goodness and toward nothing but power and domination of others.

The longer James continues his life in music, the more he senses he is heeding the call to co-create with God. Mary is not just someone he composes music about. For James, Mary is a subject, a living force who can enter into his subjectivity, thereby inspiring his creativity and directing his talents toward a cultural and civilizational renewal.

James understands his creativity as akin to the divine breath of the Creator that reaches out to human genius. The creative inspiration always begins with God. With inspiration, a human person experiences an inner illumination that brings together the sense of the good and the beautiful and awakens energies of mind and heart, which enable one to conceive an idea and then give it form in a work of art. This understanding of divine inspiration is what Pope John Paul II meant when he wrote in his 1999 "Letter to Artists," that "every genuine inspiration, however, has some of that tremor, that breath with which the Creator Spirit suffused the work of creation from the very beginning."[18]

Music, Modernity, and the Search for the Sacred

The temptation to sever human creativity in the arts from the religious quest is a temptation that can be found not only in secular philosophies but also at times in some religious thought. In his writings on music, theology, and the arts, James has repeatedly warned that the so-called self-liberation from tradition and religion that some say creative artists need in order to be free is an illusion. So-called self-liberation often leads to an abyss of darkness.

To be "clever"—that is, to intentionally break rules of tradition simply for the sake of rebelling—has led to a secular music environment that seems to be delighted to produce music that most people would deem inaccessible. Is it any wonder then that such music that deliberately aims to reject tradition fails to reach people outside certain inner circles of composers? James fears that seeing music as not needing any purpose outside itself with which to connect makes this beautiful art purely cerebral and lacking resonance. In his own journey, by going deeper into his Catholic faith, he found divine inspiration and true creative freedom. James warned that if the craft of composing music is detached from the human search for the sacred, we will end up with a superficial mysticism that lacks any grounding in the world or the transcendent.

Despite having had the most exceptional experience of grace known in the history of mankind, to bear Christ in her womb, most of Mary's life was ordinary. Mary's humility stands as a stark contrast to the myth of the creative genius who either finds inspiration wholly within himself or asserts himself as a kind of "priest" for all of society, claiming to have taken the light from God (or the gods) and now must be revered as a prophet. In the Gospels, Mary is often to the side; she walks alongside Christ but does not detract from him.

Although James sees the search for transcendence and spirituality all throughout modern culture, he asks, "in what sense can we call a spirituality made in our own image, to suit our own comforts, to fit our own schedules and agendas, transcendent of anything?"[19] As Maritain warned and as James has seen in the modern music world, rejecting tradition but embracing rootless mysticism leads to obscurity, not inspiration or illumination. Christianity, James insists, must be incarnational: as Christ took flesh in Mary's womb, along with Mary, we are called to be vessels of the grace of the Incarnation, infusing the divine spirit into matter. Receiving an inspiration from the Holy Spirit carries a responsibility to share the light, such as by fashioning beautiful things out of formless matter.

For James, the revival of sacred music, especially among secular people who are searching to connect their spiritual longings to a religious tradition, is an opportunity to communicate the timeless message of Christianity about God's mercy, sacrifice, and redemption. After the interviewer called his views of divine inspiration *avant-garde*, James reflected more deeply on how the Christian view of creativity stands above what he calls the "transient fashions and banalities of the culture of today."[20] Perhaps drawing on his interviewer's words, he now says that "a brave radical countercultural vision that a creative person can have is to attempt to resynchronize the world around us."[21]

Music as a Bridge and Well

It was a sunny day in May 2019, and we stood at the top of a hill at a graveyard in the Bronx, where John Aroutiounian, a former student of mine from Yale, had been born just twenty-six years earlier. Just hours earlier I had found the courage to deliver a hopeful eulogy about John: I knew John had willingly accepted his death with hope in eternal life. But in that moment, the finality of his death hit me hard. I felt unconsolable.

I started in disbelief as his coffin was lowered slowly into the grave. Suddenly, someone began singing the Salve Regina. A melody of lament and of hope rose up to heaven, as we slowly we chanted this hymn in Latin (translated here into English):

> Hail, Holy Queen, Mother of mercy,
> our life, our sweetness, and our hope;
> To thee do we cry, poor banished children of Eve;
> To thee do we send up our sighs,
> mourning and weeping in this valley of tears.
> Turn then, most gracious advocate, thine eyes of mercy
> toward us;

and after this our exile, show unto us the blessed fruit of
thy womb, Jesus.
O clement, O loving, O sweet Virgin Mary.
Pray for us, O Holy Mother of God,
that we may be made worthy of the promises of Christ.

That heavenly chant helped me glimpse a new vision of reality where the veil between life and death is pulled back.

Less than twelve months later, tragedy struck the same family again. John's father died of COVID-19, right when lockdowns started. We could not gather for a funeral to grieve together. I was unmarried, living alone, and isolated.

The night I learned that John's father had died, I kept chanting the Salve Regina in Latin while sitting alone on my couch.

Suddenly I heard voices inside my head, singing with me. *Was that John? His father? Angels? Was I imagining this?*

The voices continued. They were not intrusive nor loud. I initially resisted but then embraced the supernatural presence surrounding me.

The voices were harmonious. Gentle. The voices were so beautiful that somehow, they expressed both the pain and the joy in my heart.

At rare times such as this occasion when I heard voices singing with me, that special gift of sacred music to lead to an intimate encounter with the divine is so apparent. The great traditions of sacred music contain chants, words, and melodies that I can repeat countless times, preparing me to find hope once again in those moments when am I dumbfounded with grief, or all alone in a chaotic worldwide moment, or both.

Mary as a Gateway to the Eternal Now

I have gradually understood more deeply why recovering the joy of both making music and hearing beautiful music, of both sacred music and popular folk music, is important for churches, homes, and shared culture. Sitting in the recording studios at BBC Scotland with James for a public conversation on theology and music that aired in November and December 2025, I commented that at the heart of the modern longing for a sacred experience through music, as well as at the heart of James's wisdom about Mary as an inspiration for creatives, are the questions of human freedom and human happiness.[22] I rubbed rosary beads on my lap while I mustered the courage to share the words that came to my mind when I prepared my remarks for that conversation. I shared that thinking about musical analogies for faith reminds me that human freedom can't be autonomy from God lest it produce cacophony. What if we lived our lives as if each of us is a line in a melody? Music calls to us. We respond freely to God's call, harmonizing with him. Yet, we move to our own beat as we go from tension to wholeness. Sometimes we lose our way due to our weakness, and we turn back, harmonizing ourselves inside and out once again.

James remarked to me afterward that the revival of sacred music is a powerful way of presenting to secular audiences who are also music lovers, like listeners of BBC Radio 3, the timeless message of Christianity: God is merciful, he sacrificed his son for our redemption, and we can return our own acts of sacrifice and lift up our own acts of creativity in gratitude and rejoicing.

In the life of faith, we are bound together by something bigger than all of us that allows us to develop our personalities, explore our talents, and be led by our desires to something attractive. My unhappiness comes from ruminating, judging, and competing that takes me away from Christ. My obsessive focus on myself feels like a powerful trap. I need to trust in God's mercy, not my own perfection. In this daily spiritual battle, Mary is a subject in my life, not an object. Her inner life, her subjectivity, is open to all of us. And she opens the door to the heart of God. She is the reed of God.

Mary's freedom, openness, and receptivity to the Spirit can be a powerful inspiration for artists today. Musical analogies help draw out how James and I have both experienced Mary's calls in the depths of our hearts, pulling us into a divine drama. But what can it mean to co-create with God, to use our gifts creatively and beautifully, not with a superficial, banal, flashy cleverness? Each of us, in following our creative inspirations, whatever our personal vocation may be, can encounter Mary who always walks with us, inviting us, not commanding us, to be creative, to have courage, to be faithful and let the Spirit into our bodies.

As James writes, Mary "is not only an example and a model for all Christianity, but in this is the embodiment of what human beings experience only dimly: that we live with ambiguity of limitation and creative possibility in constant tension. She opens the door to the very heart of God, and in the silence of my own contemplation, in that necessary stillness where all composers know that music mysteriously begins, the following words from our sacred liturgy have lodged themselves in the womb of my soul, trapped in a scarlet room, gestating gently with a tiny distant pulse: Hail Mary, full of grace."[23]

Chapter 7

"Am I Worthy?"

Tammy Peterson Follows Mary to Jesus and the Church

Am I Worthy?[1]

About five years before I met her, Tammy Peterson was diagnosed with an advanced stage of cancer. There was little hope for survival, so her doctors advised her to prepare for the end. Knowing her mother and other relatives had succumbed to cancer in their early sixties, Tammy saw no reason why her fate should be any different.

"When the doctors told me I had ten months to live," Tammy shared, "I simply accepted it as my destiny."

She went home and shared the prognosis with her son with detachment, passing on the simple message, "I'm going to die."

But her son's reaction moved something deep inside her. "I saw a look of pain in his eyes that no mother wants to see." Tears filled her eyes as she remembered this pivotal moment. "My son's face mirrored all the love I had given him. And suddenly," her eyes widened as she recounted that unforgettable moment, "a feeling of worthiness lifted the weight of the world off my shoulders. All my cynicism simply vanished.

Seeing his love reflected back on me, I could love myself more for the love I had shared with him. The sacrifices I had made as a mother were meaningful to him, and that meant I was worth saving."

She was overcome with the realization that just as her son loved her, God loved her, and her life was worth saving. "I knew this sudden change in me came from God because I'd already made up my mind that I was going to accept the prognosis. Really. I had no hope. When the body dies, that's it, I thought."

Looking back, Tammy believed that, until that moment of unexpected grace, her guardian angel had been protecting her, holding her tight so that she did not fall into total cynicism. "I just felt my self-doubt disappear and the Holy Spirit filled by body. I knew it was grace because I was filled with a sense of peace that I had never before experienced."

Her perspective on her prognosis changed radically.

Tammy was now convinced that her life was *worth* saving, but her destiny—to live or die—was not under her control. "Only God knows when I'm going to die," she said. "God has so powerfully entered my life that I knew it was simply my responsibility to pray and ask that God's will be done. I experienced a tremendous freedom to just know that my duty was just to seek God every day and let him be in charge of whether I live or die."

Tammy opened up about her life with me during our first podcast together in July 2024. I shared with her how, even among people with no formal religious belonging or belief, time and again I heard a sense that, even in their state of near desperation, they felt a human capacity to connect to something sacred. My past work with people who had abused alcohol or drugs led me to meet people who longed for a sense of worthiness coming from something transcendent, something outside of themselves. There is a spiritual reality that can't be reduced to a mere psychological desire but expresses a conscience, a mysterious place we connect to a reality outside ourselves, a sense that our lives are worthy just because we exist.

I froze on the screen when Tammy blurted out with a sudden urgency, "When I was diagnosed with terminal cancer, I wondered: Am I worth saving? Not really." She was eager to discuss with me her journey from cynicism to hope, and how Mary had led her to Jesus and to the church.

Just about a month before my first podcast with Tammy, our mutual friend and collaborator, the iconographer Jonathan Pageau, took me backstage after one of Jordan Peterson's speaking engagements as part of his "We Who Wrestle with God" speaking tour. Most people lined up to say hello to Jordan, who was wearing one of his bold jackets covered in icons of Mary. Jonathan eagerly introduced me to Jordan's wife, Tammy, who was standing in a corner wearing mostly dark, muted colors of clothing. As he introduced me, Jonathan handed her one of my previous books on beauty and told her I was writing a book on Mary.

Tammy greeted me with a warm smile and spoke in a soft, gentle voice. I shared my interest in Mary, including the many visual representations of her in sacred art. After a few minutes, Tammy grabbed her phone, took my number, and immediately texted her podcast manager to schedule a public conversation with me on Mary.

I was so intrigued by Tammy's conversion story and her wisdom about prayer and the spiritual battle against pride that I asked her if I might come visit her sometime just to share more about our journeys and pray together.

Surrender

The dramatic coming of the Holy Spirit into Tammy's body, and her sudden conviction that God's will would be done—whether that be for her to live or die—intrigued me. Tammy shared more about her upbringing in a mostly non-practicing Protestant family in Alberta, Canada. When she was a little girl, she learned about Christian prayer at home and occasionally attended church. Tammy distinctly recalled rejecting Christianity when she was thirteen. An older relative had introduced her to yoga at that time, and she embraced it and sustained a regular meditation practice for decades. At the time, Tammy felt no need to hold on to Christian traditions or prayers; in fact, at college and art school, she encountered so many philosophies that claimed we can be fulfilled and happy without Christian revelation or traditions that, for most of her adult life, she barely thought about Christianity. Tammy married Jordan, raised their children, learned massage therapy, and practiced holistic forms of healing, focusing on natural remedies and Eastern meditation.

But when her life hung in the balance and she was confronted with her deeply ingrained doubts about her worthiness that were suddenly overturned by the coming of the Holy Spirit into her body, she recalled basic Christian prayers. Repeating those simple prayers placed her in relationship with God with an intimate dialogue while she endured excruciating pain.

Tammy described in detail the uncertainty about her survival. "The surgery got the cancer, but when they took out my lymph nodes, they left a hole. Because the fluid accumulating in my body was very painful, they put a shunt in my abdomen to drain the fluid." The result was that her bodily fluids were draining, depriving her brain and her body of nutrients.

Tammy began to lose weight. Even if she ate, she nonetheless was starving to death: she dropped from 120 pounds to 85 pounds. Recalling her realization that this could be the end, Tammy described how "my shoulder blades stuck straight off my back. You could see all my ribs. When I looked at myself in the mirror, I thought, 'O geez, this looks like the end of life.'"

But despite being near death, Tammy was not afraid. The mysterious encounter with the Holy Spirit led her to put her life in God's hands. "I was just there, doing what I had to do."

Her blood pressure dropped so low that they tried a few different cuffs to measure it and barely got any blood pressure reading. "My electrolytes were way out of balance, and you need potassium and calcium for your heart to pump, and so if your electrolytes are too out of balance, you can have a heart attack."

Each day, teetering between life and death, Tammy had to summon the strength to endure more tests, more scans, more treatments.

"I knew I needed to pray, so I repeated the Lord's Prayer," she told me.

"You just started praying the Lord's Prayer all of a sudden?" I asked in surprise.

Her grandmother had been a practicing Christian, and she

had learned the prayer as a child. She was grateful for having a set prayer coming out of a long tradition. She contrasted her sudden eagerness to pray the Lord's Prayer to the kind of meditation she had done in yoga, which she characterized as emptying her mind.

In contrast, returning to Christian prayer she described as seeking God's will, not her own, and immersing herself in specific prayers that had sustained others through time. "In yoga," she said, "there's no text, no Scripture. I knew I needed the Word of God, so I just repeated the Lord's Prayer." Repeating this simple yet profound prayer led her to realize the significance of sharing a set prayer with others across space and time. "These prayers had sustained people who were really searching for God," she remarked. "There was something powerful in the repetition of a simple prayer. Praying sustained me. Saying the Lord's Prayer was a very tangible way of rising above the pain and the discomfort and the fear."

As she had suddenly turned to Christian prayer for the first time since being a teenager, I wondered how her heart responded to the words she repeated. In the hospital, with a lot of time alone, and a lot of time fighting back fear and pain, Tammy explained that as she repeated the Lord's Prayer line by line, over and over again, she questioned herself as to whether she believed what she was saying. She understood enough about Christianity to know that prayer is a dialogue with God, so she turned the repetitive words into a conversation.

"I would say, 'Our Father who art in heaven, hallowed be thy name,' and then I would ask myself, 'Do I believe these words?'"

Her face brightened as she recalled this internal conversation where the words she repeated helped her form a relationship with God. "And from within me came the response: 'Yes, I believe I have a Father in heaven who is good and holy!'"

"'Thy kingdom come, thy will be done,'" she recited. "Letting go of control was no longer an option—it had become a requirement. 'Yes, of course, God's will must be done.'"

"'Give us this day our daily bread.' Yes—I knew my sustenance depended on God."

In those simple words, repeated again and again, Tammy's deepest need, even deeper than her physical survival—her need for worthiness—was met by the certainty of a good, holy Father who forgave her and sustained her.

"'Forgive us our trespasses.' My heart swelled with contrition. 'Yes, I must understand what I've done wrong. Please forgive my trespasses!'"

Her focus did not have to rest on her emaciated body as her heart was lifted up to contemplation of God's presence in her body and soul. God's forgiveness and mercy were particularly consoling to Tammy.

In addition to the Lord's Prayer, Tammy learned the Jesus Prayer: "Lord Jesus Christ, Son of God, have mercy on me, a sinner." That simple prayer of acknowledging our brokenness and asking for God's help gave her fortitude because she was not relying simply on herself any longer. When she felt afraid, she would simply say, "Jesus, I trust in you."

Tammy's grandmother had taught her the Serenity Prayer, which she recalled often as her life hung in the balance: "God, grant me the serenity to accept the things I cannot change;

courage to change the things I can; and the wisdom to know the difference."

Up until that point in her journey, Tammy's sudden openness to Christianity had come mostly from memories of prayers she had learned when younger. When a Catholic teacher from Toronto whom Tammy barely knew began visiting her in the hospital and offered to pray with her, Tammy joyfully welcomed a companion in her prayers.

Specifically, her friend taught her a contemplative practice with repetitive prayers called the rosary.

"I had somehow heard of the rosary, but I didn't know how to pray the Hail Mary prayer. I was curious about Mary. I even recalled as a young girl looking for Mary at my local Protestant church and not seeing her. As a little girl, I really wondered: Where is the mother of Jesus?"

I was surprised that Tammy could recall so distinctly looking for Mary at her childhood church. Why might that be? I probed.

Tammy insisted that her longing for a close relationship with Mary just seemed like a natural desire. "I was looking for a relationship, a mother-son relationship between Mary and Jesus, but I didn't see it at our church," Tammy replied.

Every day for weeks, her new friend prayed the rosary with her in the hospital, teaching her how to meditate on Christian Scriptures while doing so.

Tammy learned all twenty mysteries of the rosary, which are divided into four sets of five reflections that chronologically traverse the life of Christ in the Gospels: the Joyful, Sorrowful, Luminous, and Glorious Mysteries. Some of those Gospel passages—notably, the Annunciation, Visitation, and birth of Christ—directly refer to Mary, while most others focus on the life of Christ: his suffering, preaching, transfiguration, death, and resurrection.

In his book *Lessons in a Rose Garden: Reviving the Doctrinal Rosary*, theologian Aidan Nichols, O.P., explains how praying the rosary is meant to "focus the imagination on the tableau—the icon—of each mystery, asking from God the grace to penetrate it, to understand it."[2] The rosary is normally prayed while holding on to what looks like a necklace with five sets of one large bead and ten small beads, plus a dangling crucifix and one more large bead and three small beads. While holding on to the crucifix, the rosary starts with a recitation of the Nicene Creed—the statement of faith agreed upon by early church fathers. Then, one large bead and three small beads hold a place for one Our Father and three Hail Marys, which are prayed while asking for the grace to grow in three theological virtues: faith, hope, and charity.

For weeks on end, Tammy's friend visited her daily to pray the mysteries of the rosary, reading short mediations from different mysteries of the Gospels and then meditating while slowly repeating a set of prayers. For each large bead, one Our Father is recited, followed by ten Hail Marys on the small beads, and one Glory Be while holding on to the fabric between the small bead and the next large bead. Each of those cycles is called a decade of the rosary (for the ten Hail Marys) and each set of mysteries consists of five decades of the rosary, plus the opening prayers. The rosary concludes with the Salve Regina, Hail Holy Queen.

Although normally it would take around twenty minutes to pray on set of mysteries of the rosary, Tammy and her friend often prayed together for one or even two hours as her friend encouraged Tammy to really ponder the meaning of each Gospel scene. The five Gospel passages that make up The Sorrowful Mysteries, for example, moved Tammy deeply to picture Jesus's brutal death. Those five sorrowful mysteries are called: the Agony in the Garden (Matthew 26:39); the Scourging at the Pillar (Matthew 27:26); the Crowing with Thorns (John 19:5); the Carrying of the Cross (Luke 23:28); and the Crucifixion (Luke 23:46).

"I realized that not only was Mary tenderly loving Jesus as a baby," Tammy remarked. Her sacrificial love for her son provided a deep insight into Mary's motherhood of Jesus and Jesus's love for his mother. "When I pictured Mary at the foot of the cross, I thought, 'Oh yeah, now they are together for sure.'"

Tammy had willingly sacrificed her own desires to raise her son. She had been by his side as he faced many challenges, and her son offered back to her his love, his gratitude for her sacrifices, when she faced a likely death.

"Through the rosary, I pondered how Mary was there at Jesus's birth and his cross," she said.

When her friend suggested that she offer up her prayers for others, Tammy rejoiced at the chance to sustain others with her prayers, just as she felt the prayers recited by other Christians past and present were sustaining her. "My family was holding me up. I felt like if I prayed for them, I was doing something for them. I was so grateful to be able to pray for others."

The more she named specific intentions, the more her desire to pray for others grew. She thought of what she could pray for, expanding her prayer intentions beyond her family and including acquaintances and strangers.

"I started off praying for people close to me, but then my prayers became more universal," she said, explaining how "I asked to pray for *all* mothers in the world. For *all* the fathers in the world. Let's pray for all those who are dying. I prayed for all those who don't have faith."

Using bodily images to illustrate the internal change she experienced, she remarked how, "my body weight was decreasing, but my heart was expanding."

After months of uncertainty with her health, months in which she was sustained in prayer and growing in a sense that she was, indeed worth saving, in a manner no one can explain medically, one day, her fluid simply stopped leaking. Tammy's health suddenly improved. What had been deemed incurable was now pronounced cured. Though she would bear bodily scars from the procedures she had undergone, Tammy's life was no longer in danger.

She went home, now with a new set of questions: How would she maintain the Christian prayer practices she had taken up while her life teetered in the balance? What did it mean to really give her heart to Jesus, and was she ready to do it? Did she need to belong to a church in order to sustain her faith in Jesus? Now that she had a second chance at life, what was God calling her to do?

Trust and Transformation

When I flew to visit Tammy for three days in Toronto during a long weekend in August 2024, I eagerly perused her husband,

Jordan's, psychology books that filled numerous bookshelves in the living room. Tammy led me to the sunroom at the front of the house, which had previously been where she did yoga meditation every morning and now was transformed into a place for Christian prayer, adorned with sacred images to guide her focus.

Tammy showed me where she normally sat each morning to pray the rosary: a comfortable chair positioned to let light stream in through a stained-glass window she had installed years before. A few books sat on the table next to her chair: a Bible and a couple of devotional texts. Around the chair hung an icon of an Old Testament prophet. She had hung a crucifix depicting Christ on the cross that had been a gift to her. Her prayer corner also featured an image of Mary pictured as Our Lady of Guadalupe that she brought back from Mexico City, and an image of St. George slaying the dragon, a symbol of Tammy's ongoing spiritual battle with pride.

"When I left the hospital, I really wasn't sure where my journey would lead. I had left the church when I was young. I rejected the authority of the church. But I knew it was good to pray." As she had been practicing yoga meditation daily for decades, Tammy described that it wasn't difficult to now do daily Christian prayers. But, she explained, "What changed was the purpose and focus."

The steps in her ongoing conversion were not as dramatic as either the coming of the Holy Spirit into her body when she delivered her diagnosis to her son nor the consolation that had sustained her while repeating the Lord's Prayer and praying the rosary while in the hospital. But Tammy was convinced that a regular prayer practice was necessary for her happiness and ongoing discernment.

"I had to admit I didn't know what I was doing, and I needed God's help. I was unchurched for a long time. It took me a long time to come to the humility that it takes to have a prayer practice."

Each morning, Tammy started her day with the rosary prayers. Like when she was in the hospital, she prayed for her intentions—for the needs of her family, for strangers, and for her own struggles with anger and resentment. She asked God for guidance, to help her see the next right thing to do.

"Whether I was angry, resentful, or fearful, I can take that to prayer in the morning with Mary. I can take all my concerns through the Gospel stories while praying the rosary. I was so happy to learn to pray the rosary because it gave me such better direction, a very clear direction in life. It wasn't up to me to know everything. When I'd finish my prayers, I'd have a new perspective. Then I could take the next right step, trusting in God."

Inside of her, Tammy felt that lightness she had experienced at her dramatic Pentecost moment continuing. She felt lighter now knowing that she no longer had to figure things out for herself. She grew in confidence that God would show her the way.

"Before, I was lost. Trying to figure it all out on my own was like a path to hell for me. But now, if I pray, I'll eventually see the way forward." Learning to pray daily helped Tammy develop patience. "Sometimes it takes a day, other times it takes a month. But it's magical when suddenly you see the sign, and you know what to do."

Drawing on images from nature to explain how prayer helped her discern, Tammy remarked that, "praying is like being guided by the stars on the open sea. Suddenly a storm comes, and you can't see the stars. You are in the dark. But if you have a prayer practice, it's like a small little light is still there. At first it is hardly anything. But you just keep praying that the light grows. So, you strap yourself to the mast and just try not to sink. Eventually, the stars reappear, and you can see your way forward."

Tammy contrasted her new life led by prayer with her previous life, in which she focused on doing her duty. When she was younger, she rejected the authority of the church and most forms of authority. Instead, she learned to assert her willpower. Rather than her identity connecting her to any kind of a tradition, she rested in the power she could harness inside herself to do things. She "powered through" hurdles in life, whether it was pain as an athlete, completing schoolwork, fulfilling paid work, or carrying out her duties as a mother and wife.

"I was kind of a drill sergeant to myself," she remarked. Carrying out her duties gave ger a sense of autonomy. But to find worthiness, she needed a relationship with God.

Tammy's exploration of the Christian Gospels helped her see her most intimate family relationships not just as a series of exchanges based on obligations, but as sacrifices, a willing offering for the good of another based on love.

"The home is supposed to be place of nurturing and service to each other. I am a mother, someone who has sacrificed for her kids. But until the Holy Spirit entered my body, I had questioned my own worthiness. I didn't realize that the sacrifices of being a mother pleased God."

Tammy slowly accepted Jesus in her heart because she could see that he, too, was part of a family. The Christian story appealed to her because God comes to us through sacrificial love. "I started to see how Christianity is based on a sacrificial relationship. Jesus preaches the Gospel and gets into trouble with the authorities. And he gives up everything. And Mary is there to stand beside him and not protest. Mary observed the crucifixion of her son; he is the sacrificial lamb. But he doesn't leave his mother alone; from the cross he asks that his mother be cared for by the apostles." Jesus's love comes to us, at least in part, through the great sacrifices his mother made to give birth to him, raise him, and follow him to the cross.

The more she prayed to Mary in the rosary, the more she longed not to follow her own will but God's will for her life. "My life got more meaningful and more challenging when I decided to follow God's will. My ideas were nothing compared to what God has planned."

What seemed to be missing from Tammy's life, she now recognized, was that she herself needed a Savior. "When I began praying the rosary, I felt uneasy about the notion of Jesus as my Savior. But the more I searched the Scriptures, the more I realized my life had to adhere to the Word of God. Without that guidance, I'd be lost."

Strapping herself to Mary through the rosary every morning, asking for light, Tammy shared that, "my journey back to God, to the church, and to Jesus, began with Mary. The daily prayer with the rosary made the Gospels real to me. Mary brought me to Jesus through the rosary because the rosary is really a meditation on Gospel stories."

I was honest with Tammy that her entrance into the Catholic Church had surprised me. "I listened to some of your earliest podcasts," I said. "You said you wanted to pray personally as a Christian, and you wanted a Christian community. But you also said you didn't want the authority of a church."

Knowing that not everyone who suddenly falls in love with Gospels, has a dramatic encounter with the Holy Spirit, or reveres Mary, decides to commit to joining the church, I asked Tammy what had changed for her.

First, she referred to her longing for community and friendships with other people who prayed. "Just like I welcomed my friend to visit me at the hospital with gratitude, I just started saying yes when other people like you offered to visit me and talk with me."

When someone offered to introduce her to a Catholic priest who could answer her questions, she agreed. Tammy confessed that as a young woman, she had rejected various forms of authority, having witnessed their misuse. "I had seen so much abuse of authority that I was skeptical of authority."

Tammy accepted the guidance of the priest to help her understand what Christians believe. He gave her a copy of the Catechism of the Catholic Church, which is around seven hundred pages long (with many references to writings of the church fathers and a detailed Scriptural index). She felt free to express her hesitations, and he thoughtfully answered them, directing her to different parts of the Catechism when appropriate. The Catechism is organized around four major sections: The Profession of Faith, The Celebration of the Christian Mystery, Life in Christ, and Christian Prayer.

As she studied the words and meaning of the Nicene Creed, her heart was increasingly engaged. "The Creed is a simple yet profound statement of faith. It gave me joy to affirm each and every single line. I really believe what the Creed says is true."

Her conversations with the priest covered intellectual questions, but he also challenged her to ask herself what God was saying to her in the depths of her heart.

In particular, the priest asked her to pray about why, given her enthusiasm for the Gospel, the Nicene Creed, for Mary and her need for a community of believers, was she still hesitant to give her heart to Jesus?

"He encouraged me to scour my conscience, to think about my sins from the past that might be holding me back from a deeper relationship with Jesus," she told me. Then, gently crying, sitting with me in the same prayer corner of her home where she had daily prayed the rosary since coming home from the hospital nearly five years earlier, Tammy told me, her new friend, that she had held on to sins from her past that made her feel unworthy of Jesus.

Tammy longed for a deeper freedom than "doing her duty"; she wanted spiritual freedom that comes from receiving God's sacrificial love. The priest guiding her helped her to see that—whatever might be holding her back, Jesus died for *her* sins so she could be free. She wanted to accept God's mercy that came to us through Jesus.

Slowly, day by day, step by step, the light attracting her to Jesus and to the church grew stronger and clearer.

Acknowledging her own sins was one fact that changed her views of authority. As she humbly admitted her own sins, she realized that others' imperfections should not keep her from approaching the church. "Even if you don't like your clergy or local church for some reason, you can't let that stop you from saying, 'I've missed the mark. I've sinned. I need guidance.'"

The awakening of her conscience, her need for repentance, led her to a greater awareness of Christ's love. Although the priest answering her questions, and the explanations of the faith offered in the Catechism where important, Tammy's decision to enter the church was a response to a personal call.

Simply put, Tammy said, "Christ was calling me. I had been away from the church for a long time. It took a lot of humility to come back. But in my heart, I knew it was time to return to the church."

Tammy needed what she called the tools of the church to help sustain her prayer, and she accepted that to be a Christian means you need guidance. "I needed to be rooted somewhere. I was searching for belonging." About five years after her dramatic encounter with the Holy Spirit, Tammy was welcomed into the Catholic Church at Easter 2024.

But the unity between Jesus and Mary was central to her understanding of what the church is. "It's so beautiful to see in my local Catholic Church that Mother Mary is there behind her son on the cross. She is the church. Mary is that belonging."

Show Me Your Love

But after having hosted me in her home, attentively listening to me discuss the endless lists of theology books I had read,

Tammy's gentle, kind demeanor moved me to open my heart about a powerful moment of healing my damaged self-worth.

As an intellectual, I am often more comfortable describing my faith through elaborate explanations of human nature, the workings of grace, and the persistent problems of evil that cry out for hope in a good God. Rarely do I talk about my own Pentecost moments—surprising moments of grace where my body and soul, heart and mind, seemed to be healed in an instant. Those moments of grace, the absolute certainty that I did not create those experiences because the change was so strong, have always been a light for me in the dark seas.

I first learned of the Pentecostal movement in the Catholic Church through research for my book on Haitian Catholicism. When I tried to be an outsider, an observer at a Haitian Pentecostal healing service in Montreal, I largely succeeded. As I watched and listened, the leader of this small group prayed over each hungry soul looking for Christ's healing. Somehow, he could read their spirits. His prayers for each person were unique and specific.

"Would you like us to pray over you?" he asked.

I squirmed in my seat. But I couldn't find the heart to say no. When their hands descended on me, I tensed up and cried out inside my heart, "I'm not worthy!"

To my amazement, the leader named the bonds holding me back. Although he did not describe exact details, he was close enough that there was no way he was just randomly guessing. His description of the bonds holding me back were quite different than the other people he had prayed over.

Nothing dramatic changed that night for me, other than I

was less skeptical of Pentecostal forms of Christianity, at least for other people.

A few years later, I was deeply troubled by sadness, regret, and anger following my father's death and a romantic heartbreak. Nothing I tried to let go of my sadness seemed to work. Desperate for some relief, I called a friend who was in a Catholic Charismatic group.

"Wow, funny you should call today. There's a healing service tomorrow night at a college campus where I'll be playing the music," she said.

Initially, I said I couldn't make it, as I wanted to attend a theology lecture. Suddenly, it dawned on me: Why was I resisting?

The next night, I awkwardly walked into a small chapel at a local college, not sure how to act. A Catholic priest, Father Robert DeGrandis, and a Protestant minister, the Reverend Betty Tapscott, led the service. Their message was simple: anger and resentment hold us back from receiving the love of Jesus. No matter what injustice you have faced, no matter how broken your heart feels, no matter what sins you have committed, God wants to set you free spiritually.

People of varying ages and backgrounds were kneeling, crying, listening, and longing. I wept gently, recalling all my regrets, self-pity, and anger.

Then, for some reason, my hand felt like it was burning. I fought back a nearly uncontrollable desire to grab the hand of the lady next to me. Was I just looking for touch to ease my pain? I shoved my hand in my pocket. "This is SO weird. Stop it!" I chided myself.

Suddenly, the woman next to me turned and looked at

me with a gentle smile. She opened up her hand and said, "I brought this medal from Medjugorje [a site of Marian apparitions in the southern part of Bosnia and Herzegovina]. Do you want to hold it?"

I grabbed it out of her hand and clutched the medal as we all knelt and prayed a forgiveness prayer that lasted nearly twenty minutes.

We were then each invited to come up to the front for healing prayers. I hesitated. I watched others receive a blessing and fall down. This time, my unworthiness didn't hold me back.

I walked up the aisle and stood in front of Father DeGrandis, gently closing my eyes and picturing Jesus healing me. I was ready to let go of all that was inside—what I could name and what I still couldn't put my finger on. I knew more than ever that Jesus wanted to heal me, if I let him. I witnessed how these two ministers had special powers to share that healing love, and with gratitude for their ministry, opened myself to let Father DeGrandis lay his hands on my head.

When Father DeGrandis prayed over me, I felt an incredible tension leave my body, just like Tammy had described at her Pentecost moment. I felt lighter, almost floating above the ground. I knew in that moment that something had broken inside of me. I knew that my life henceforth would be different. Although not all my wounds were healed in one instant, never since have I felt the kind of emotional pain I had when I walked into that room.

As I drove away, I put on my favorite CD of a Christian band. But it was silent. I figured that my CD player was broken. Suddenly, the silence was punctuated by a final song to Mary that came at the end of the CD. I had never let the silent pause be there long enough to hear the slow, repetitive chant, "Mother Mary, come to me. Mother Mary, help me. Mother Mary, show me your love."

The Visitation

Before I left Tammy's home in Toronto in the summer of 2024, our conversation returned to the daily battle with pride and ego that keeps us from accepting God's will in our lives. For people like me who put so much pride into career success, it's very hard to accept that my sacrifices and losses, not just my achievements, are meaningful to God. Coming to see that we cannot earn our worthiness had been crucial for both of us. We each were grateful for being forgiven, and for the sense that along with the gift of faith comes a responsibility to offer our efforts back to God.

When Tammy asked me about my daily prayer practices, I shared with her how David and I pray in our home prayer corner, filled with David's icons of Mary, saints, prophets, and Jesus. We generally follow the order of morning prayer and evening prayer from what is referred to as the Liturgy of the Hours. The regular cycle of those prayers includes chanting the daily Psalms, the Lord's Prayer, making prayers of petition, and reciting the Magnificat, Mary's words from Luke 1:46–55 that Tammy and I had heard earlier when we attended Mass together in Toronto.

When Tammy and I attended that Mass, we heard the Gospel reading of the Visitation (Luke 1:39–56). Picturing

Mary and Elizabeth during the Visitation resonated deeply with our shared longings to trust in God and find strength not through our own power but through humility and through a relationship with God lived out and through a church community.

Why are we not always moved by the presence of Christ in Mary's womb, just as Elizabeth was when Mary called on her? Although she had just been asked to become the Mother of God, Mary did not exalt herself when Elizabeth greeted her as the "mother of my Lord" (Luke 1:43). Mary knew that her worthiness came from her unique relationship with God. By giving Mary to us as the mother of our Lord, God wants us to remember that he desires a bond with us as intimate as that of a mother with her unborn child in her womb.

In her meeting with Mary carrying Christ in her womb, Elizabeth referred to Mary as "blessed" not just once, but *three* times in those Scriptures.

"*Blessed* are you among women, and *blessed* is the fruit of your womb" (Luke 1:42).

"And *blessed* is she who believed that there would be a fulfillment of what was spoken to her from the Lord" (Luke 1:45).

Elizabeth rejoiced, knowing that the blessedness of Mary's womb is a sanctuary open to all of us. John the Baptist leaped in the womb, recognizing the Messiah had come.

Mary returned all these words of praise back to God. In the Magnificat, Mary responded to Elizabeth, saying: "My soul magnifies the Lord, and my spirit rejoices in God my Savior, for he has regarded the lowly estate of his handmaiden" (Luke 1:47–48).

But I still struggle to trust in God's plans. Hearing Tammy's story reminded me of my Pentecost moments, when I have become keenly aware that my body is temple of the Holy Spirit. I often join an online fellowship with Tammy, where women from various faith backgrounds acknowledge our faults, resolve to live up to our standards better, accept that God has power over our lives, and resolve to take the next right step with courage. No matter when we accepted the calling to journey towards God, we can all support each other.

To counter my pride and self-pity that leads me to lose my peace so easily, Tammy encouraged me to send her a daily list of things for which I am grateful to God.

"Don't forget to be grateful for the struggles," Tammy once reminded me in an email. "We aren't in control; our responsibility is simply to pray and ask that God's will be done. None of us knows how long we have to live. We can just start each day by offering ourselves to God and trusting in Him completely."

Conclusion

"Am I Not Your Mother?"

The Drums Began

Around midnight, the drums began. One by one, people moved into the circle's center and started dancing to the beat. I knew that in Vodou, different drumbeats called down different spirits.

The Mambo, the master of ceremonies, you might say, seemed to be guiding the participants, helping them to connect with the spirit world. A few times, he held the participants as they started to shake or move, a sign that a spirit was entering their body.

In 2001, I spent a week in Haiti as part of an intensive summer course on Haitian culture, language, and religion. At the time, I was learning about Haiti as part of my PhD in sociology at Princeton University. When our trip to Haiti scheduled a stop at a Vodou festival, I tried to adopt the approach that my discipline encouraged to all forms of religion: that of a neutral, outside observer.

But little did I imagine that I would struggle to be just an onlooker. As the dancing became more frenetic and people waved their arms in the air, I began to sweat profusely. Why did my body feel hotter at midnight at this Vodou ceremony than it had during the full August sunshine? One of my tour guides, herself a Vodou practitioner, came up behind me and sprinkled Florida Water on me, a kind of water used for purification in Vodou. My skin sizzled, like oil dumped into a hot frying pan.

Then a woman, dressed in red and who looked about eighty years old, threw herself down in the middle of the circle. She began crawling backward faster than I had ever seen anyone crawl forward. She was possessed by the serpent spirit.

I watched in amazement at this clearly supernatural occurrence. Suddenly I felt like someone had punched me in the stomach. Had a spirit entered my body?

"I'd like to have a supernatural power like that," I thought, wondering how it would feel to defy the laws of nature.

A moment later, one of the other students on my trip, a Haitian American named Jeremiah, came up to me. Trembling and sweating, he leaned forward and quietly asked me, "Do you think this is devil worship?"

My first reaction was to try to maintain a façade of neutrality, a charade that I was not feeling any spiritual presence. "It could be," I admitted. "But I don't know for certain."

"Well," he said, clearly searching for an excuse to depart, "you look very uncomfortable. How about we just leave?"

Neither of us was truly neutral. But neither of us wanted to admit to the rest of the group how troubled—or, at least in my case, attracted—we were to the inexplicable events unfolding before our eyes. We each looked to the other for an excuse to exit.

Our fellow travelers informed us later that following our departure, the rituals became more intense. The Mambo was clearly possessed by a spirit, as his face was contorted. One half of his face was squished, and the other half was not. More people gradually joined the circle, as I had been tempted to do. They danced, called on the spirits, and, in turn, were possessed by spirits. Before their eyes more and more the *lwa*, the god-like spirits, entered into human bodies, directing their movements and words.

And then the animal sacrifices began. To a strong beat, with ever more people dancing, the Mambo took a giant knife and killed a goat. Then, he wiped blood from the dead animal on the knife and used the bloody knife to slaughter a lamb.

At that point, all the members of our tour group—with one exception—begged to be taken away. It's one thing to read about bloody animal sacrifices to the gods and another to witness them.

Later, in a quiet, lush garden full of palm trees, exotic flowers, and delicious fruit, Jeremiah and I shared our reflections on what had happened. As a Catholic, I noted how the Vodou ceremony we attended took place the night of the vigil of the Assumption of Mary, which is celebrated annually on August 15. As a Haitian American Protestant Christian, Jeremiah had always been steered away from any celebrations involving Mary precisely to discourage Christians from confusing veneration of Mary with worshiping one of the goddesses of Vodou.

Recalling Al Raboteau's work about slave conversion to

Christianity, I shared with Jeremiah how Christians worship God alone. In communal worship, we venerate the saints because we consider them to be like family members, people who have gone before us in faith and who are spiritually present to us. The saints are not seen as demi-gods, but witnesses. Saints are our ancestors in faith whose example we seek to imitate and whose ongoing presence among us we celebrate. The saints have received entrance into the kingdom, something we anticipate as our own destiny.

When I published *Faith Makes Us Live*, I was challenged by some who said Haitians' love for Mary was simply masking their Vodou practices. But the people I wrote about knew that Mary is not a goddess with power in and of herself. Nor is she a Promethean figure, somewhere elevated above humans, a demigod who steals power from the gods and comes down and joins us humans, turning her back on God.

For the faithful Haitian Catholics I had come to know, Mary is never in competition with Jesus; she's a human being, a mother, and a bridge to the divine. But she herself is not divine. Her humble submission to God's will elevates her through his grace.

I spent the morning quietly in the peaceful garden at our hotel in Haiti, praying the rosary, asking Mary to protect me from evil. I confessed to Jeremiah that the temptation I experienced at the Vodou ceremony heightened for me that I could never let down my vigilance in spiritual battle. Dropping in and out of Mass attendance and praying only when I needed something was not enough to fight my own version of rationalism and disenchantment. I realized that I was vulnerable to deceptive spiritual powers pounding at the door of my heart.

My head knew better, but I needed help. Like a child, I turned to my mother's mantle for protection.

The Call You Never Want to Get

Little did I know that in less than twenty-four hours after I fled the Vodou ceremony, I would be thrown onto an emotional roller coaster. In the ensuing weeks, I was called to fight another sort of evil: my struggles to forgive others and to forgive myself.

One of the tour guides in Haiti came running up to me.

"Margarita," she said, her voice trembling, "your aunt just called my cell phone. Your father had a stroke. He is undergoing surgery right now. You had better call her right away."

I ran to the lobby of the historic Hotel Olofsson in Port-au-Prince to make a collect call.

My aunt's gentle voice told me, "You had better come home today. Your father might not make it."

All flights leaving Port-au-Prince that day were full. I begged my way onto an Air France flight to Miami, where I spent the night at my aunt's house.

At 2 a.m., the phone rang. "Please pray right now," my brother said somberly. "The doctors just told us they are trying to save Dad, but they aren't sure they can."

I faced a total abyss. Would I ever see my father alive again? Would I get to say goodbye?

I collapsed on the floor, all alone, sobbing and shaking. I grabbed my rosary. Pain shot up and down my leg for no apparent reason. Memories flooded my mind. I called out to my father across the distance, saying the things I wished I could say to him in person. I journaled the prayers, Scriptures, and thoughts that came to my head. I was searching for God, feeling desolate, finding no sleep, no inner peace, and not knowing what the morning would bring.

Suddenly an image, as if illuminated by fluorescent light, jumped off the wall before my eyes. The image depicted a sailor at the helm of a boat, with Jesus standing calmly behind him, guiding him. Then I glanced over at the crucifix on the wall. On my bedside table, I noticed a picture of the Mother of God with the baby Jesus.

I pictured Mary at the foot of the cross as Jesus suffered. "Our Holy Mother understands the dark night," I scribbled in my journal.

Memories of my father flooded my mind. I was grateful for how much he had educated me at home, buying me all the used books I ever wanted to read. He taught me math; we started with addition and subtraction and moved on to long division. When I was five, he even taught me the basics of algebra. During family meals, he hung a giant poster of the periodic table of the elements and a world map next to our kitchen table, quizzing me and my brothers on science or geography. I got one dollar for every A I got in school. I got one extra dollar if I turned a B into an A.

Dad wanted me to do things boys normally did. I helped with the yard work. I helped change the oil in our car. I was often the only girl who played on local children's basketball and teeball teams. Dad made family photo albums of our visits to national parks and historical sites. Every December, I sat next to him and dictated my part of the family Christmas letters.

My father had been deployed to Vietnam in 1969, just months after marrying my mother in November 1968. I later found out that he had won several medals for valor in life-threatening combat, including a bronze star medal. As a young man, my father was strong and smart. He had always been a voracious reader, a history buff, and a math genius with a sharp sense of humor. But Vietnam had changed him. He came back a chain smoker. Ashes from unfiltered Philip Morris cigarettes filled our house and car. After his military service in Vietnam, he stopped practicing the Catholic faith in which he was raised. He cursed more often.

Sometimes when our playing got too loud, my father became angry. Sometimes he would hit one of my brothers. He yelled at my mom, and sometimes he hit her, too.

I'll never know why, but, even if I did something wrong, my father never hit me or raised his voice at me. But I recalled many times sitting alone in my room as a child, scared as I listened to my father yell at my brothers or my mom. A few times, when my dad flew into a rage, my mom called the police to defuse the situation. After the worst incident when I was eight years old, my mother moved out of the house to a domestic violence shelter.

My father begged her for forgiveness and pleaded with her to come back, promising he would never lose control again. After a few weeks, my mother returned. Home life was never perfect. None of us ever forgot the painful moments. But we had hope, we loved each other, and we tried our best to move on. My mother always emphasized the many positive things my dad did for us.

Now that I was in my late twenties and about to lose my

father, I begged God to let him survive long enough for me to say in person what my heart had long known: that I forgave him.

My father survived the night. Over the next few weeks, he barely clung to life. He was intubated and going in and out of consciousness.

Sitting at my dad's bedside, with tears rolling down my face, I told him he scared me when he got angry, and, a few times, when he got violent, I would hide in my room. I also thanked him for how he educated me, teaching me mathematics, geography, and baseball.

"Dad, I forgive you." His green eyes welled with tears. I continued, "I know you love me and never intended to hurt me." He softly nodded his head.

Then, I prayed out loud the Our Father. When I reached, "Forgive us our trespasses, as we forgive those who trespass against us," I added, "God forgives all of us, Dad. Don't be afraid. He has mercy on you."

Not long after, my family gathered at my father's bedside. We prayed the rosary and cried as we watched Dad take his last breath.

Greater Darkness, Greater Light

The day after my father's funeral, the alarm rang at 6:15 a.m. I splashed water on my face and dragged myself to the car to drive my brother to the Ronald Reagan Washington National Airport. I returned home and slept—the best sleep I had in a month. But, all morning, I missed panicked phone calls.

When I finally woke up at noon, I found out that two

planes had hit the World Trade Center, one around 9:15 a.m. and the other around 9:45 a.m. The Twin Towers fell. Then a third plane hit the Pentagon, which I had driven in front of at sunrise just hours earlier. A fourth plane had crashed in a field in Pennsylvania.

It was September 11, 2001.

I felt numb. I couldn't cry. It was as if events were happening around me, but a wall blocked the emotional impact of those events. Perhaps I was in shock. I had no idea what to do, say, or feel.

On the afternoon of 9/11, I walked to our local Catholic parish. I sat in silence in church as many people came and went, crying, lighting candles, saying prayers, and hugging each other. A priest celebrated Mass, offering the Eucharistic sacrifice for the dead and their loved ones.

Thoughts raced through my mind. How could God allow such suffering? What was I to do now with my life? Nothing seemed worthwhile. The more I thought about everything, the less certain I felt about anything.

I had no clarity. At home, I tried to write in my journal. I searched for words of hope, praying the Psalms. When I climbed into bed, I clutched my rosary and repeated Hail Marys until, exhausted, I finally fell asleep.

I went to grief therapy. But I found no comfort when the therapist encouraged me to talk about bad memories and express my anger. I desperately wanted healing, not just for the pain my father may have caused me but more for all the ways in which, having lost my father, my own failings screamed at me mercilessly. All my mistakes flooded my mind. I felt like a terrible daughter of my earthly father, not to mention an unworthy child of God. I longed for a place where I did not have to face my own failings.

I judged myself harshly, perhaps. But my emotional pain was debilitating. My mind was clouded with recriminations, fears, and inadequacies. I genuinely believed that that I'd never experience true joy ever again.

Our Lady and Haitian Catholics

A few months after my father's death, I recovered the energy to complete my dissertation. I returned to Miami and spent about six months living in the guesthouse next to Notre Dame d'Haiti Catholic Church. It was there that I met people like Stephanie, whose words of love and forgiveness after experiencing such horrible violence in Haiti I had shared with Al Raboteau and anyone who read my book *Faith Makes Us Live*.

When I published my book in 2009, I had hesitated to tell people how much I was personally touched by the people I met. But Stephanie's joy helped me to believe that God's love is indeed stronger than hate. If God forgives even the worst injustice, how could I hold on to such hatred for myself?

During my time at Notre Dame, I rarely spoke about my struggles. But I often wept in private. Certainly, God's grace flowed to my heart through the witness of the people I met. I joined ladies like Stephanie in praying the rosary at Notre Dame in Miami. They had such gratitude to God; they prayed first and nearly exclusively for others' needs. I was obsessed with thinking about myself. I acted as though, if I prayed more for myself, God would obey my wishes.

Embodied rituals for Holy Week at Notre Dame d'Haiti that I had never seen in my local Catholic parish helped take me out of my self-centeredness in prayer. For example, on Good Friday, I walked in the two-hour procession around Miami's neighborhood called Little Haiti. As several people reenacted Jesus's walk to Calvary, the rest of us sang hymns like, "O Croix, tu règnera; O Croix, tu nous sauvera." (O Cross, you will reign, O Cross, you will save us.)

Marching through the heat and singing with members of the congregation, I did not experience a quick fix for my emotional turmoil. But I did learn how to engage in spiritual warfare. I experienced how powerful it is when we bind ourselves in community rituals, imploring Mother Mary to heal our wounds and plead with us before God to help us see his face.

Part of my spiritual battle has always been that I long to escape the cross. I want to have new life in Christ without carrying the cross. That Good Friday at Notre Dame, we ended our outdoor procession by venerating the cross on our knees. At the foot of the cross was Mary, the mother of compassion and mercy. Jesus left me his mother from the cross to strengthen me; she was with me as I embraced the cross and my heart cried out in hope of forgiveness of my sins.

The Cosmic Battle Between Good and Evil

In December 2024, a message from Evan, whose "wild Marian experience" in Ireland I detailed earlier in this book, led me to ponder Our Lady and Haiti. Evan texted me that he had just read an article in the *New York Times* about the killing of nearly two hundred people in Port-au-Prince, apparently in retaliation by a gang leader who believed someone had put a Vodou spell on his son.

"It is quite astonishing that such a dark and seemingly superstitious thing can have such power in our 'modern' age," Evan commented.

"There's a lot more beauty in Haiti than is conveyed in the news," I shared. "The Haitian Catholics I know love Mary, and they implore her protection. They firmly believe that Mary is, among other things, the woman who crushes the head of the serpent in Revelation. She can protect us against evil."

I then told Evan how I learned during my trips to Haiti that I, too, need to turn to the Mother of God for protection. Of course, Jesus has triumphed over evil on the cross, but his mother protects and shields us.

"In this cosmic battle between good and evil, we have a Savior, Jesus. And our Savior has a mother, Mary, who is a prayer warrior."

I have long hesitated to share the story of the Vodou ceremony lest I paint only a partial picture of the richness of Haitian culture and beliefs. But there's no question that part of the reason why I wholeheartedly embraced a relationship with Mary as my spiritual mother is that she can help us in the battle against evil, whether that be against evil spirits that tempted me at the Vodou ceremony or my own pride that tempts me constantly.

Under My Mother's Mantle

To turn Evan's attention away from violence or evil spirits, I shared with him words Mary spoke to St. Juan Diego on

Tepeyac Hill five centuries ago. I had never read—much less pondered in my heart—Mary's words to St. Juan Diego until James MacMillan told me how he set them to music for a priestly ordination.

> Listen, put it into your heart, most little of my sons: Let nothing frighten or grieve you, let not your heart be disturbed, do not fear any sickness or anguish. Am I not here, who am your Mother? Are you not under my protection? Am I not your health? Are you not happily within the folds of my mantle, held safely in my arms? Do you need anything more? Let nothing else worry you, disturb you.

James set Mary's words to music for a choir with a baseline sung in Latin, which (in translation) repeats, pulling us into deeper harmony with Mary, who reaches out to embrace us:

> Holy Mary, most tender of virgins, receive the constant prayers of your little servants: raise up the fallen, correct the wayward, strengthen the trembling, comfort the faint-hearted: so that we may ever offer praises to you whom we honour as the Mother of the Most High God.

Listening to a recording of the music, I was filled with that enveloping sense of warmth, serenity, and gratitude for my spiritual mother. I hoped Evan would be similarly inspired by Mary's presence among us always, as he had been at the well in Ireland.

Mary Is My Mother

As I matured in life, it was humbling and challenging for me to admit that I needed anyone to guide me, not just a priest or a spiritual guide, but also a spiritual mother. I wanted to do everything myself. I thought I could solve every problem, take charge of all things using my head or hands.

But going on pilgrimages to Marian shrines like Lourdes and Fátima and witnessing others humbly asking for Mary's protection and intercession made me wonder: Why not throw myself down on my knees and pray the rosary, asking for healing and help? So, many times, I did.

Did I experience any miraculous healings, whether that be physical injuries cured, the dead being brought back, or the reconciliation of a relationship that left me with a broken heart? No, I did not. At least not in the way I expected.

But I did experience peace and joy, knowing my happiness doesn't depend on me. I grew closer to God not by avoiding suffering, but through it. I learned that my happiness lies in opening myself to receive, not in what I achieve. God encounters us in unexpected ways, not the ways we often demand.

The faithful through the millennia believed in Mary's spiritual motherhood. Today, Mary's spiritual motherhood is a refuge of tenderness and hope for countless people such as those in this book. Not all people I've written about here were even necessarily looking for her, but Mary called to them, and they opened their hearts to her as their spiritual mother.

Why is Mary a prism through which we can come to see God's unexpected gifts of grace at work in so many ways? Although we could look to many different people in Scripture or church history for examples of hard work and sacrifice,

Mary has the unique role of being the mother of God. Her life is inseparable from the life of Christ, not only at the moment of his birth, but throughout his life on earth. She continues to transmit to us the joy of our salvation.

Yet in a world shaped by scientific rationalism, many Christians—including me—hesitate to speak of Mary's spiritual motherhood, fearing they might be accused of superstition. Even among friends who shared my faith, I concealed my deep personal relationship with Mary behind academic analysis. But as more people came to me to share their profound intuitions about Mary, their longing for her spiritual maternity, I realized that my hesitations about sharing my love for Mary were a disservice to those who wanted to hear my personal reasons for loving Mary and learn from me about how Mary can be a bridge to other aspects of the Christian faith. As with those I wrote about in this book, knowing Mary better has tied me closer to the church, to Christ, and to the Trinity. Knowing Mary has helped me to know and accept myself, to see my life as part of a mysterious and beautiful plan even when things do not go my way.

Mothers remind us that we are known. We are loved. We are cared for. We all have a deep longing to be known, to approach God as we did as children with open hearts. Mary is both a powerful mystic who discerned God's mysterious call to her, and she's an ordinary mother who raised a child.

Mary is certainly a model of virtue, and a disciple of Christ to be emulated. But Mary's perfect cooperation with God's grace does not make her just an "ideal" figure against whom we measure ourselves, and strive, and fall short, and keep striving—as I often do when looking at the saints.

Christianity is about much more than rule-following. The Christian faith is about openness to inspiration, to being led by the Holy Spirit to become uniquely who we are called to be. The verbs associated with Mary in Scripture, such as listen and ponder, convey deep, slow, intuitive movement. Nouns associated with Mary, such as a garden, point to depth, humility, and patience. Mary is not just a model of discernment; she helps bring us closer to God so we can hear his calls to us.

Mary's living presence among us is expressed through musical terms like "fugue," which conveys movement that involves repetition, interweaving, and bringing together. As a mother, she understands our need for her patient love to guide us; like a mother, she loves us not only when we were knit in our mother's womb but also as we move towards God, becoming more intertwined with her and the body of Christ, thereby bearing Christ to others as she does. Mary actively protects and guides her spiritual children, helping us to find the courage to be what we are called to become.

Analyzing Mary isn't sufficient. We are called to truly know her and, through knowing her, to know her son and, consequently, to know ourselves as God intended. Learning how others have encountered Mary and what that means for their faith journey offers us a myriad of ways to ponder Mary's presence in our lives, calling us to the love of the Trinity. We can come to know Mary through those who have known her, through our intimate prayers, through the words of Scripture, and through sacred art and music venerating her.

Too often, polemics about various elements of Christian doctrine related to Mary have prevented Christians from knowing her personally. Mary is not just a name, an object, or an artifact of history we discuss when having doctrinal discussions, as important as those may be. Mary is a living person in whom the meaning of Christian doctrine is exemplified.

The more I have integrated Scripture, art, and music into how I share my love for Mary, the more she becomes a living person truly present in my relationships with others. Reflecting on Mary at Pentecost, one student I taught concluded that his main insight about Mary was simply that, as he put it, "she was there." For example, he noted that "Mary's final appearance in Scripture is one that is quiet, yet theologically profound for our understanding of who she is. In Acts 1:14, it is written that after the Ascension, the disciples returned to Jerusalem and 'were constantly devoting themselves to prayer, together with certain women, including Mary, the mother of Jesus.'"

She is not mentioned by name when the spirit descends, "but her presence is assured," he wrote, and "her presence is no mere coincidence. Mary is a figure who is present, not only at the birth of Christ, but at the birth of the church itself. Mary stands at the threshold between Incarnation and the church, between the overshadowing of the Spirit at Nazareth and the outpouring of the Spirit at Pentecost."

Born into a Protestant family in the Midwest, that student remarked how, "in a culture that prizes visibility and accomplishment, Mary's presence at Pentecost affirms that God's Spirit moves just as powerfully through those who remain, pray, and trust. Mary stands as an example with those whose faith is quiet and whose discipleship is marked by waiting."

Perhaps what struck me the most was his call for all

Christians to take Mary into their homes, as surely the first disciples did. "Mary is not a theological obstacle or denominational boundary marker," he noted, "but a witness to how the church itself is formed. Mary reminds us that the Spirit who overshadowed her at the beginning continues to shape the church through ordinary faithfulness. By reclaiming Mary in this way, pastors and educators can offer congregations a deeper, more spacious vision of discipleship: one rooted not in fear or controversy, but in Scripture, humility, and hope."

Why is Mary not only unfamiliar to many Protestants, but as he put it, "fraught with danger?" Sadly, he noted that Mary "often appears as a boundary between different denominations and traditions rather than a shared witness within the Christian story. Concerns about idolatry, excessive devotion, and perceived displacement of Christ have led many mainline Protestant communities to sidestep Mary almost entirely, mentioning her only briefly during Advent before returning her to the margins of faith and spiritual practice."

As I noted in the introduction, people long for Pentecostal moments. That may be one reason why the Protestant silence about Mary is approaching an end. As this student put it, "this silence carries its own theological cost. When Mary is removed from Christian imagination, we lose something essential. We do not only lose something about Mary herself, but also about the nature of discipleship, incarnation, and God's way of working through the lowly and overlooked."

Mary was there at Pentecost, and she is with us now, whether we recognize her or not, guiding us to a deeper understanding of the mysteries of faith. For example, another student I taught reflected how "Mary's response and receptivity toward grace is an image of creation itself, when purified and properly redeemed by God." Because she accepted her divine calling, she is "an icon of the world to come, a window into the divine life, displaying the true and ultimate freedom that is only found in Christ." By reflecting on "the person of Mary and the development of doctrine surrounding her, we see how Mary magnifies God's plan for all of creation." Although prior to taking my class, this student knew relatively little about Mary, he reflected how "now I see how Mary can serve as a model for Christians to imitate, always ultimately looking to Christ for our devotion."

Learning about Mary's presence in the lives of the faithful makes me want to be more like her—patient, listening, serving, and forgiving. The more I'm like Mary, the more I can rejoice in all things. Knowing Mary reminds me that the church is a body of people, a communion. Pondering Mary's faith reminds me that God is a Trinity, three divine persons communicating love.

Like Evan, who experienced Mary's warm embrace at a healing well in Ireland, I want to ponder what God is doing in my life. Mary is a mystic. She hears God's word and lets it draw her deeper into prayer, and she responds with love. If we let her, she will help us be mystics, too, people open to mystery—people like Evan with the courage to pray always, even if apparently nothing happens.

Al Raboteau reminded me that there is no joy in Christianity without the cross, something Mary knew more than anyone. Her compassionate gaze comes to me through the liturgy—whether that be on Sundays or special processions during

Holy Week—reminding me that we pass through this vale of tears to be transformed into the joy of the resurrection.

Sally's heart-wrenching losses of three children in her womb reminded me, as she put it, that God breathes life into dead things. Sally's encounters with Mary reminded me that our freedom is not just something we use to make choices; our freedom means we take risks. We put our lives in God's hands, as Mary did, and step out in courage.

Aidan Hart's burning desire to make sacred art and teach about how that sacred art restores the dignity of the person in a culture drowning in superficial materialism encouraged me in my longings to encounter God through embodied forms of beauty. As he told me, many people are used to worshiping with white walls or have been misinformed that all sacred art is merely idolatry rather than a window to a divine encounter. For seekers and lifelong people of faith, authentic beauty opens our heart to God.

James MacMillan's revelation that he hears echoes of the Annunciation everywhere resonated in my mind, stirring my heart as the beautiful music he composes does. Music allows me to share the beauty of God's presence with others. One day, I put on James's choral music for my brother and sister-in-law, whose daughter is severely disabled and does not speak. She blinked her eyes, smiled, and turned her head to hear the music. I believe she heard angels in James's music, as I once did while chanting the Salve Regina hymn to Mary. When, upon hearing James's music, my sister-in-law exclaimed, "this music makes me want to bow down and worship," I resolved to keep sharing beautiful sacred and choral music in as many ways as I can.

Tammy Peterson's call to return to the Christian faith through Mary's motherhood does not fit a kind of rapid conversion story that goes, "I was lost, but had a 360-degree turn all in one bright day and knew what path to take." Rather, Tammy's initial encounter with the Holy Spirit was followed by long spells of darkness. She slowly learned Christian prayers and practices she relied on every day, every instant, to stay the course during her painful hospitalization. She reminded me that even if we realize in an instant that our lives have worthiness, that does not mean we also know what to do next. It means we live each day with the certainty that Christ has saved us and made us worthy of his love, no matter what. He gave us his mother, and the authority of the Church, to guide us and help us sanctify our loves and make our sacrifices into a song of praise.

The Highest Honor of Our Race

Evan and I spoke about Our Lady of Guadalupe just days before her appearances are celebrated in the church calendar on December 12. My heart weighed heavily that day in 2024, as I was worried about my mother's ailing health. Having relied on my mother for five decades, the tables were now turning. My mother needed my practical help and my prayers.

When I walked into St. Paul's in Princeton, where I had knelt at daily Mass so many times with Al Raboteau, I walked straight up to the image of Our Lady of Guadalupe surrounded by flowers. I knelt, laying all my burdens down.

In silence, walking in a straight line down the central walkway, the St. Paul's schoolchildren came in wearing their uniforms, the same uniform I had worn at St. John the Evangelist Catholic School in Frederick, Maryland. The students from kindergarten to eighth grade, children of Asian, Latin American, African American, and European heritage, filed in and took their seats in the pews.

The priest, dressed in a robe featuring Our Lady of Guadalupe on the front, processed down the aisle as we sang the same song I had once sung as a school child, "Immaculate Mary, Your Praises We Sing." Quoting the angel Gabriel in Luke, echoing the mystery of the Annunciation, and reflecting the opening lines of the Hail Mary prayer, we cried out in the refrain, "*Ave, ave, ave Mariiiiiia!*"

The priest's opening prayers brought us into the presence of Jesus and the Holy Spirit. The congregation recited the Gloria, a prayer of gratitude and adoration to the Most Holy Trinity.

Then, a young girl around age twelve read Zechariah 2:10, "Sing and rejoice, o Daughter of Zion; for lo, I come and I will dwell in the midst of you, says the Lord."

We sang the Psalms of the day, along with a refrain that says: "You are the highest honor of our race," a creative adaptation of Judith 13 set to music to honor Mary.

A young boy, around eleven, read us the Visitation narrative from which the Hail Mary prayer draws several lines. "Blessed are you among women, and blessed is the fruit of your womb! And why is this granted me, that the mother of my Lord should come to me?" (Luke1:42–43).

Catholic Mass is always centered on the Eucharistic sacrifice. By surrounding the sacrifice of Christ with Scriptures and songs that remind us of his mother, Mary, we joyfully recall how Mary's gracious "yes" at the Annunciation brought our Savior into the world. Mary was present at the foot of the cross. Mary shares in the life of the Trinity, the greatest gift God has given us, the source of our dignity. Mary's name thus appears in various parts of the liturgy because her presence is a part of salvation history.

Mary's centrality to the faith is underscored by her title as the Mother of God and the ancient practice of calling her the New Eve. Celebrating Mary's appearance as Our Lady of Guadalupe, the mother of the Mexican people, reminds us that Mary is truly present to us today, in ordinary and extraordinary ways. Sometimes she stirs my heart with hopeful inspiration as I sit in the garden praying the rosary; other times she protects me, giving me fortitude in the face of a seemingly impossible situation.

Suddenly, I was so moved by the celebration that I let go of my analyzing and my worrying. Tears filled my eyes as I watched the children on their knees singing beautiful songs to Our Lady of Guadalupe, surrounded by roses, just like she was on the *tilma* and in the stained-glass window we had restored in my mother's home church in Cuba.

I cried. And cried. I just wanted to be a little girl trusting in my mother as I once was, a girl who loved Marian processions and the rosary. My mother loved Mary, and my mother loved me, her only girl, and she called me "her shadow."

Our Lady's words to Juan Diego kept coming to me in Spanish, the language of my biological mother, the language of my heart: "*No soy yo tu madre?*"

Am I not your mother?

Why are you afraid?

Why was I crying? I wanted those children to know, as I did when I was a child, that Mary was their mother. I didn't want them to grow up and forget her.

I don't always remember my mother Mary, but my childhood memories of her filled me in that moment. I'm grateful I went to a Catholic school; I'm grateful that my mother taught me to pray the rosary at home; I'm grateful I memorized Marian songs as a child. Honoring Mary in the prayers at Mass that day sparked in me a deep sense of connection to my mother Mary, reminding me that, even if we forget her, she doesn't forget her children.

My tears represented both repentance and joy. I felt sorrow for my weakness, my drifting from home. And I felt gratitude for my mother Mary's *tilma*, her mantle, which holds me together just as Tammy's guardian angel held her until she was ready to accept the Holy Spirit into her body and soul.

No so yo tu madre? Am I not your mother?

I drafted a reflection that concluded with this prayer:

"Inner peace, safe harbor, Mother Mary, hold my hand. Help me to trust again. I have strayed, but I want to belong again. Teach me to love."

Teach Me to Suffer and to Hope

Although my mother and I don't pray the rosary together as often as we used to, my mother thanks me often for inspiring her to continue that practice she learned as a child in Cuba and then passed on to me. Now, with each mystery of the rosary, she looks up an image from the Scriptures. To aid her in prayer, she also plays music. And she recalls the music of her childhood.

One day, she sang to me in Spanish for several minutes a song called "Enséñame a Sufrir." Teach me to suffer. At her boarding school in Havana, they would walk into the courtyard daily and pray before a statue of Our Lady of Fátima. We couldn't visit her school when we went to Cuba together, as it has been converted into a medical school. Where images of Jesus and Mary once hung, images of Fidel Castro and Che Guevara now cover the walls. Slogans of the Cuban Revolution, like "fatherland or death," have replaced the motto of the Sisters of the Sacred Heart of Jesus who founded the school: "One Heart and One Soul in Jesus."

My mother speaks more frequently of her physical ailments. She has accompanied several of her thirteen brothers and sisters through their final moments in this world. Although it hurts me to see her ailing health, Mary seems more present than ever to both of us. My mother gave me the gift of life, an example of tender love, and taught me the faith. As she enters the middle of her eighth decade of life, her relationship with Mary has flourished in new ways which I trust are preparing her for God's will in her life.

Now, as my mom reflects on the fact that her final days are numbered (as they are for all of us, I remind her), she has told me, "Thank you for bringing me back to my hometown in Cuba. Thank you for bringing me back to my mother, Mary."

With Mary holding our hands, I believe love will conquer evil. I know the battle to maintain Christian hope will not end until I face my final days. In every spiritual battle, I implore Mary to take me under her mantle and protect me.

In the meantime, whether I suffer or rejoice, I call out to Mary with the ending of Hail Mary prayer, "Holy Mary, Mother of God, pray for us sinners, now and at the hour of our death."

Amen.

Annotated Bibliography

This bibliography serves as a guide for those seeking to deepen their knowledge of Mary from Catholic, Orthodox, and Protestant Christian traditions. The conversations I had with the people I interviewed for this book were deeply influenced by what I learned from the readings below about Marian theology, devotion, and scholarship. I hope this bibliography invites readers to continue their exploration of Mary across the rich landscape of Christian traditions, both past and present, and to recognize Mary's presence in both the Old and New Testaments, the history of Christianity, their personal devotion, and liturgical worship.

Readers interested in topics not included here, or those wishing to explore specific subjects in greater depth, will find numerous additional bibliographic resources in each of these books, as well as in most theological libraries. The St. Andrews Encyclopaedia of Theology is a free online resource that features short essays from leading scholars on various theological questions, including many covered in this book. The Catechism of the Catholic Church is also available as a free online resource. Many of the papal documents referenced can be found on the Vatican's website. The Internet Archive provides free versions of many writings by the church fathers.

I have organized these works into the following sections: Scripture/Biblical Studies; Early Church; Systematic Theology; Spiritual Classics; Cultural, Social, and Historical Perspectives;

Art and Music; and Ecumenical Perspectives. I placed the books in these categories based on their dominant themes, though nearly all contribute to more than one category.

Scripture and Biblical Studies

Barker, Margaret. *The Mother of the Lord. Vol. 1: The Lady in the Temple.* Bloomsbury T&T Clark, 2012.

As a Methodist minister and biblical scholar in the United Kingdom, Barker reveals how ancient Jewish temple symbolism illuminates Mary's role in early Christianity. Her research explores the rich biblical foundations for Marian symbolism, including Mary and the burning bush, Mary as a garden, and various other praises of Mary found in prayers such as the Litany of Loreto.

Calvin, John. "Commentary on John 2:1–11." In *Commentary on the Gospel According to John, Volume 1.* Translated by William Pringle. Christian Classics Ethereal Library, n.d. Accessed April 11, 2025. https://www.ccel.org/ccel/calvin/calcom34.viii.i.html.

In this Scriptural reflection written between 1540–1563, John Calvin, a prominent leader of the Protestant Reformation, argues that Christ's miracle at the Wedding of Cana had nothing to do with Mary's prodding. Christ rebuked her because she went beyond her proper bounds, and John recorded this incident so that we would go directly to him with our requests, not his mother. He critiques the vociferous praises of Mary as blasphemous.

Calvin, John. "CCC.—To the French Church in London." In *Letters of John Calvin: Volume 2.* Translated by Ford Lewis

Battles. Edited by John T. McNeill. Volume 7, *John Calvin: Works and Correspondence*. Presbyterian Board of Publication, 1858.[1]

In this letter addressed to the French Church in London, John Calvin advises against referring to Mary as *Theotokos* (Mother of God) because this title for her is not found in Scripture. He cautions that using such a title would reinforce the ignorance of those who hold superstitious beliefs, rather than edifying the church.

Gaventa, Beverly Roberts. *Mary: Glimpses of the Mother of Jesus*. University of South Carolina Press, 1995.

Gaventa taught New Testament at Baylor University and Princeton Theological Seminary. She portrays Mary with careful attention to historical context and literary features, aiming to promote her inclusion in Protestant biblical scholarship while writing about Scripture in ways accessible to readers from all Christian traditions. Gaventa's focus includes the Gospels of Matthew, Luke, and John, as well as the Acts of the Apostles.

Luther, Martin. "The Magnificat." Translated by A. T. W. Steinhaeuser. In *Sermon on the Mount and the Magnificat*. Volume 21, Luther's Works. Edited by Jaroslav Pelikan. Concordia Publishing House, 1956.[2]

Martin Luther's reflections on Mary's *Magnificat* were written as a reflection to Prince John Frederick, Duke of Saxony, around 1520. Luther extols Mary's human virtues and holds her up as a model for rulers and all the faithful to follow in her humility, diligence, hard work, and listening to God. Mary only glorified God and would oppose any treatment of her as an idol. He affirms Mary as the Mother of God, explaining that the title refers to God's power to do mighty things. To call upon Mary so that God's work may be done is perfectly acceptable to Luther.

Pitre, Brant. *Jesus and the Jewish Roots of Mary: Unveiling the Mother of the Messiah*. Image, 2018.

Pitre is a Catholic biblical scholar who offers an accessible yet scholarly examination of Old Testament typologies and prophecies, highlighting Mary's role in salvation history. His work connects Mary to Old Testament figures such as Eve, Sarah, Rachel, and Esther, as well as symbols like the Ark of the Covenant. This book clarifies Mary's title as the New Eve and explores other Marian titles with scriptural references and interpretations.

Early Church

Athanasius of Alexandria. *On the Incarnation.* Translated by John Behr. St. Vladimir's Seminary Press, 2011.

This foundational fourth-century treatise examines why Mary's physical motherhood of Christ is central to the doctrine of the Incarnation: the union of the divine and human in Christ.

Gambero, Luigi. *Mary and the Fathers of the Church: The Blessed Virgin Mary in Patristic Thought.* Ignatius Press, 1999.

This comprehensive survey of early Christian writings about Mary, authored by a Catholic, provides essential historical information on the development of Marian doctrine and devotion, including hymns, from the early centuries of Christianity. This book illustrates the principle of *lex orandi, lex credendi*, which translates to "the law of prayer is the law of belief."

John of Damascus. *Three Treatises on the Divine Images.*

Translated by Andrew Louth. St. Vladimir's Seminary Press, 2003.

Written during the eighth-century iconoclastic controversy, this fervent defense of sacred images establishes the theological foundation for Christian iconography and painting, including images of Mary. John Damascene contends that since God became visible in Christ through Mary's flesh, portraying Christ and his saints in art is not only permissible but also essential for Christians to experience Christ, Mary, and the saints as people present with us still.

Maximus the Confessor. *The Life of the Virgin.* Translated with introduction and notes by Stephen J. Shoemaker. Yale University Press, 2012.

This seventh-century biography of Mary aims to provide a comprehensive narrative of her life, drawing on non-canonical scriptures such as the Protoevangelium of James. This book discusses the early church's liturgical calendar feasts honoring Mary, such as the Dormition of Mary—which is not mentioned in the canonical Gospels but is celebrated as a feast in many Christian churches.

Systematic Theology

Bouyer, Louis. *Woman and Man with God: An Essay on the Place of the Virgin Mary in Christian Theology and its Significance for Humanity.* Darton, Longman & Todd, 1960.

This profound theological reflection examines Mary's significance in God's intimate encounter with humanity. Bouyer highlights God's humility and self-emptying in the Incarnation. He explores the mother-son relationship at the cross, depicting Mary as the Seat of Wisdom through her redemptive suffering. Bouyer, a French Lutheran minister who converted to Catholicism and became an influential figure in *ressourcement* theology, argues that Mary embodies the archetypal human response to God's initiative—a response marked by receptivity, not passivity.

Cantalamessa, Raniero. *Mary: Mirror of the Church*. Liturgical Press, 1992.

Written by a Catholic priest aiming to introduce Mary to Protestants, this accessible work firmly grounds Marian theology in Scripture while highlighting its personal and spiritual implications. He points out that dogmas are meant to explain the Bible, not the other way around. Although Mary speaks few words in Scripture, Cantalamessa stresses that Mary is the only person (besides Christ) present at the three pivotal moments of salvation history: the Incarnation, Crucifixion, and Pentecost. Her presence at these moments helps unlock their meaning. He emphasizes how Mary reflects the shared experiences of all believers and how understanding her life will help preach the Gospel of grace.

Catechism of the Catholic Church. Vatican City: *Libreria Editrice Vaticana*, 1997.

This authoritative presentation of Catholic doctrine includes significant sections on Mary that articulate her role in salvation history and the life of the church. The full version of the Catechism contains an index of topics covered, along with the corresponding Scriptural references. Particularly illuminating are paragraphs 484–511 (Mary and the mystery of the Incarnation), 721–726 (Mary and the Holy Spirit), 963–975 (Mary as Mother of the church), 2673–2679 (prayer to Mary), and 2617–2619

(Mary as the one who prays perfectly). There is no single section on Mary in the Catechism, which demonstrates that she should be understood in relation to all three persons of the Trinity. Quotations from the church fathers and scriptural references are included to indicate the origins of various teachings about Mary and the titles of Mary.

Gaventa, Beverly Roberts and Cynthia L. Rigby, eds. *Blessed One: Protestant Perspectives on Mary.* Westminster John Knox Press, 2002.

This collection of essays by prominent Protestant scholars provides theological reflections on Mary from Reformed, Lutheran, and Evangelical perspectives. The diverse contributions highlight a wide range of Protestant views on Marian theology and devotion, particularly emphasizing themes of motherhood, discipleship, and suffering.

Gregoris, Nicholas L. *The Daughter of Eve Unfallen: Mary in the Theology and Spirituality of John Henry Newman.* Newman House Press, 2003.

This detailed study organizes insights about Mary from the extensive writings of St. John Henry Newman, tracing Newman's views of Mary from his Anglican years to his Catholic conversion. Gregoris demonstrates how Newman's Marian theology exemplifies his principle of doctrinal development—authentic doctrine unfolds organically. Newman emphasizes Mary's titles as the New Eve and the Mother of God (*Theotokos*) as central to all understandings of her. Newman's thorough explanation of the scriptural and early church foundations of all Marian doctrine acts as a bridge for ecumenical understanding in our own time.

Laurentin, René. *A Short Treatise on the Virgin Mary. 6th Edition.* Foreword by Robert L. Fastiggi. The Catholic University of America Press, 2022.

This comprehensive volume on Marian doctrine was one of the final works of a Catholic priest whose work on modern Mariology included examining Mary and African Christianity. Laurentin focuses on Mary's relationship to the Holy Spirit and the communion of saints, as well as biographies of modern Catholic saints who experienced Marian apparitions, such as St. Bernadette Soubirous of Lourdes. Laurentin was also present as an advisor at Vatican II when ecumenical questions about Mary and her relationship to the church were discussed and clarified. This impressive volume covers the key questions on doctrinal development regarding Mary from the early church to the modern era. The appendices review major Marian feasts and titles and their relationship to doctrines such as the *Theotokos*, the perpetual virginity of Mary, and the Assumption.

Newman, John Henry. *A Letter to the Rev. E. B. Pusey on His Recent Eirenicon.* Longmans, Green, 1866. Reprinted by Gracewing, 2008.

In this lengthy letter, Newman defends Catholic doctrine regarding Mary from the perspective of doctrinal development. Newman, who began as an evangelical Christian in England, was ordained as an Anglican priest before converting to the Roman Catholic Church. He argues that Marian devotion evolved organically as a reflection of the early church's love for Mary, which, in turn, shaped traditions of Scriptural interpretation and doctrine. Both Newman and Reverend Pusey, an Anglican priest, were part of the Oxford Movement, a group of pastors and scholars in England aimed at reclaiming the traditions of the early church and reviving the Scriptural and liturgical foundations of worship.

Nichols, Aidan, O.P. *There Is No Rose: The Mariology of the Catholic Church*. Fortress Press, 2015.

This concise yet comprehensive overview of Catholic doctrine and devotion by a Catholic priest and theologian aims to reconcile Eastern and Western understandings of Mary. Nichols's approach to *ressourcement* theology emphasizes connecting Marian devotion to its scriptural and patristic roots while outlining its development through tradition, liturgy, and art. Much of what the West expresses in doctrine, the Eastern churches celebrate in their liturgies. In contrast to *sola scriptura* of the Reformation, Nichols takes an approach to understanding Mary using an approach he calls *totum in sacra scriptura*: the entirety of the faith is found in Sacred Scripture, but only understood fully through its expression in tradition, creeds, and the testimony of the faithful encapsulated in art, music, architecture, and liturgy.

Nichols, Aidan, O.P. *Lessons from a Rose Garden: Reviving the Doctrinal Rosary*. St. Austin Press, 2012.

Nichols seeks to recover the catechetical purpose of the rosary as a means of contemplating and internalizing Christian doctrine, rather than viewing it merely as a sentimental practice. While many perceive the rosary only as a Catholic devotional act, he illustrates how its structure and content illuminate the central truths of faith, as revealed in the Scriptural meditations that form its core. In addition to the Hail Mary prayer, Nichols clarifies why reciting the Creed, the Our Father, and the Glory Be is essential to the doctrinal rosary—Mary guides us to Christ, the Father, and the Holy Spirit. Nichols's vision of the rosary as both doctrinal and contemplative is an example of integrating theological understanding and lived spiritual experience.

Pelikan, Jaroslav. *Mary Through the Centuries: Her Place in the History of Culture.* Yale University Press, 1996.

One of the twentieth century's leading historians of Christian doctrine examines Mary's role in theology, devotion, art, and culture over the past two millennia. Pelikan was a Lutheran scholar who later converted to Orthodoxy and taught at Yale Divinity School. Topics include Mary in the New Testament, Marian typologies from the Old Testament, the doctrine of *Theotokos*, and why Mary remains central to ecumenical dialogue today. Similar to the approach in his book *Jesus Through the Centuries*, Pelikan powerfully illustrates the intersection of theological concepts, imagery, and culture throughout the extensive history of Christianity.

Perry, Tim and **Daniel Kendall, SJ.** *The Blessed Virgin Mary (Guides to Theology).* Eerdmans, 2013.

An Evangelical Anglican (Perry) and a Roman Catholic priest (Kendall) provide a concise overview of Marian doctrine and debates across four historical periods: the early church, the medieval period, the Reformation, and modern theology. Their approach emphasizes how Mary relates to Christology, ecclesiology, and soteriology, identifying both convergences and differences between Protestants and Catholics.

Ratzinger, Joseph (Pope Benedict XVI) and **Hans Urs von Balthasar.** *Mary: The Church at its Source.* Ignatius Press, 2005.

This collection of essays by two prominent Catholic theologians explores Mary's relationship with the body of Christ in the church, ensuring that a heartfelt bond of faith endures. Mary is portrayed as the foundation of the church, representing an emotional connection. Additionally, Mary is depicted as a bridge among the ecumenical, liturgical, and biblical movements in modern theology and devotion. Ratzinger's essays expertly cover extensive material in an accessible style and reasonable length.

Ratzinger, Joseph (Pope Benedict XVI). *Daughter Zion: Meditations on the Church's Marian Belief*. Ignatius Press, 1983.

In this concise, profound, and meditative essay, Ratzinger explores the biblical and theological foundations of Marian doctrine, particularly emphasizing Mary's relationship with Israel and the church. His exegesis presents Mary as "Daughter Zion"—the embodiment of Israel's faithful remnant—and illustrates how Mary reflects the continuity between the Old and New Testaments.

Saward, John. *Redeemer in the Womb: Jesus Living in Mary.* Ignatius Press, 1993.

Saward, an Anglican priest in England who later converted to Catholicism, explores the mystery of the Incarnation between the Annunciation and the Nativity, examining the theological significance of Mary's physical and spiritual motherhood. Reflecting on the gestation of Christ in Mary's womb illustrates the profound unity of body and soul.

Sheen, Fulton J. *The World's First Love: Mary, Mother of God.* McGraw-Hill, 1952. Reprinted by Ignatius Press, 2010.

This beautifully written meditation on Mary combines

theological depth with devotional warmth. Sheen, a prominent American Catholic priest and evangelist of the twentieth century, presents Mary as a model for all humanity and the most perfect of God's creatures. He illustrates how Mary's motherhood sanctifies all human love and offers insights into her role in spiritual warfare. He contrasts Mary's spiritual power with that of the sword, highlighting the close connection between human receptivity to Mary's motherly love and God's love.

Spiritual Classics

Houselander, Caryll. *The Reed of God.* Ave Maria Press, 2006 (originally published in 1944).

This spiritual classic by a Catholic laywoman from England offers profound meditations on Mary as a vessel for Christ, employing rich imagery such as the reed, chalice, and bird's nest. Mary's ordinary human life is portrayed through inspiring allegories. For instance, Houselander's poetic insights and musical analogies, like the fugue, help convey Mary's emptiness as a purposeful receptivity to grace.

Raboteau, Albert J. *A Sorrowful Joy: A Spiritual Journey of an African-American Man in Late Twentieth-Century America.* Paulist Press, 2002.

In this spiritual memoir, a renowned scholar of African American religion recounts how an encounter with a Russian icon of Mary guided his return to practicing the Christian faith. Raboteau explores the similarities between the Catholic faith of his childhood, African American Protestant religious practices—which he has written about extensively in books like *Slave Religion*—and the rituals of the Orthodox Church, where he discovered his spiritual home as a mature adult.

Williams, Rowan. *Ponder These Things: Praying with Icons of the Virgin.* Canterbury Press, 2002.

The former Anglican Archbishop of Canterbury and renowned theologian provides profound theological insights on classic Marian icons, illustrating how visual art can deepen our understanding of Scripture and guide us towards a more meaningful encounter with God. Williams's contemplative approach articulates how sacred art serves as a bridge between doctrine and personal devotion.

Cultural, Social, and Historical Perspectives

Brown, Rachel Fulton. *Mary and the Art of Prayer: The Hours of the Virgin in Medieval Christian Life and Thought.* Columbia University Press, 2017.

Brown, a medieval historian raised as a Presbyterian who later converted to Catholicism, examines medieval devotions to Mary, which flourished through the Hours of the Virgin—an adaptation of the Liturgy of the Hours tailored for Marian devotion and influential in shaping medieval Christian spirituality and imagination. Her work connects liturgical and personal prayer, highlighting the creativity of personal devotions within a structured framework of prayer hours.

Mathewes-Green, Frederica. *The Lost Gospel of Mary: The Mother of Jesus in Three Ancient Texts.* Paraclete Press, 2007.

Written for non-specialists by an Orthodox author, this accessible exploration of early texts—including a story, a prayer, and a hymn—reveals Mary as a vibrant presence in the hearts of early Christians.

Maunder, Chris. "Apparitions of Mary." In *Mary: The Complete Resource*, edited by Sarah Jane Boss, pp. 424–57. London: Continuum, 2007.

This study of Marian apparitions across history provides a scholarly and balanced evaluation of their theological significance and cultural impact.

Orsi, Robert A. *The Madonna of 115th Street: Faith and Community in Italian Harlem, 1880–1950.* Yale University Press, 2010 (Third Edition).

This landmark ethnographic study by an American social historian examines the profound devotion to Our Lady of Mount Carmel among Italian Catholic immigrants in New York during the late nineteenth and early twentieth centuries. Orsi skillfully illustrates how Marian devotion shaped community identity and moral values within the Italian American community—from which he himself hails—and how the festival incorporated everyday concerns into Marian piety.

Art and Music

Clayton, David. *The Way of Beauty: Liturgy, Education, and Inspiration for Family, School, and College.* Angelico Press, 2015.

Clayton, who was raised as a Methodist in the UK and later converted to Byzantine Catholicism, examines various traditions of sacred art used in worship, including iconography, Gothic art, and Baroque art. He explores both the form and mathematics of beauty, as well as the content within sacred art. Clayton, who makes sacred art for worship, presents beauty as essential to mystagogical catechesis, which shapes our spiritual imagination to connect more deeply with God. This book is a theological companion to his practical book (with Leila Marie Lawler) on praying at home with images, *The Little Oratory*.

Hart, Aidan. *Festal Icons: History and Meaning*. Gracewing, 2022.

Hart is a modern master iconographer who began his journey in Christianity as an Evangelical, later becoming Anglican before converting to Eastern Orthodox. In this book filled with pages of beautiful icons across place and time, he delves into the theological significance and evolution of icons for key church feasts, including several dedicated to Mary, such as the Annunciation and Nativity. Hart traced the development of icons for particular feasts in the church from the early church to the establishment of a canon of images for liturgical worship. Each chapter focuses on one major feast of the Orthodox church liturgical calendar and features numerous images and links them to Scripture readings and hymns.

Hart, Aidan. *Face to Face: The Theology of the Icon*. Gracewing, 2025.

This short book serves as an excellent general introduction to the theology, historical development, and liturgical uses of icons. This work helps connect the history of iconography and iconoclasm to the modern revival of icons not only in Orthodox but also Catholic and Protestant (especially Anglican) churches. Hart elaborates on the power of the icon to shape our spiritual vision and lives. This book is an adaptation of an article the author wrote for the online St. Andrew's Encyclopaedia of Theology.

MacMillan, James. "Theology and Music." *New Blackfriars* 81, no. 947 (2000): 16–26.

In this essay, the acclaimed Catholic Scottish composer and conductor examines various parallels between music and spirituality.

Milliner, Matthew J. *Mother of the Lamb: The Story of a Global Icon.* Paraclete Press, 2022.

Milliner earned a Master of Divinity at Princeton Theological Seminary and a PhD in Art History from Princeton University, and he teaches about Mary at Wheaton College. In this book, he traces the global influence of a particular Marian icon, Our Lady of Perpetual Help, revealing how devotion to Mary transcends time, culture, and denominations.

Vloberg, Maurice. "The Iconographic Types of the Virgin in Western Art." In *Mary: The Complete Resource*, edited by Sarah Jane Boss, 537–85. Continuum, 2007.

This brief yet comprehensive scholarly essay traces the development of Marian imagery in Western art, identifying key iconographic types and their theological significance. Vloberg examines visual representations of the typologies of Mary to demonstrate how artistic traditions have shaped our understanding of Mary's role in salvation history.

Ecumenical Perspectives

Catholics and Evangelicals Together. "Do Whatever He Tells You: The Blessed Virgin Mary in Christian Faith and Life." *First Things* (March 2009): 33–38.

This statement from an ecumenical dialogue group clarifies areas of agreement on various Marian doctrines between Catholics and Evangelicals, including the Virgin Birth. Catholic theologians and Evangelicals diverge more on contemporary teachings, particularly concerning the biblical foundations of teachings like the Immaculate Conception. Catholics have demonstrated greater piety toward Mary in the liturgy and through various devotional practices. If the relationship between specific forms of piety and doctrine is clarified, Evangelicals may also express their love for Mary as a means of leading the faithful to Christ.

Anglican-Roman Catholic International Commission II. *Mary: Grace and Hope in Christ*, ARCIC-II 580/04 (February 3, 2004).[3]

This statement clarifies vast areas of agreement between Anglicans and Roman Catholics about most Marian dogmas and devotion. Although certain differences remain, such as a disagreement about the dogmatic nature of Mary's Immaculate Conception, this statement aims to clarify misunderstandings that have exaggerated Anglican-Catholic differences about Mary in the past. Among the many areas of convergence identified are that both traditions see Mary as the *Theotokos*, as having an exalted role in Scripture, and as having an ongoing ministry in the church.

Mascall, Eric L. *The Mother of God: A Vindication of the Theology of the Virgin Mary*. Dacre Press, 1949. Reprinted by Gracewing, 2005.

Mascall, an Anglican priest, argues that Christianity without Mary is a monstrosity because she anchors our faith in the tangible reality of the Incarnation. He illustrates how to recover Mary in faith and doctrine across various denominations.

Perry, Tim. *Mary for Evangelicals: Toward an Understanding of the Mother of Our Lord.* IVP Academic, 2006.

This insightful exploration of Mary from an Evangelical perspective seeks to cultivate a biblical appreciation for her while addressing Protestant concerns about Catholic devotional practices.

Acknowledgments

This book would not have been possible without the incredible people who opened their hearts to me about their encounters with Mary. Mom, Evan, Al, Sally, Aidan, James, and Tammy—thank you.

One of the joys of being a professor is putting together a syllabus for a new class and teaching on a new topic. I thank all the students in my four classes on Mary that I have taught at Princeton Theological Seminary (PTS) for their questions, sharing resources, and going on this journey of remembering Mary with me. Guest speakers for that class on art and music included: Matthew Milliner of Wheaton College, Beatrice Kitzinger of Princeton University, Ioana Belcea (an artist in Princeton), David Clayton (my husband and an artist), and Martin Tel (C. F. Seabrook Director of Music at PTS). Martin also graciously invited me to share some of my ideas about Mary in Scripture, art, and music at a worship service for PTS students. Jessica Savage of the Index of Medieval Art at Princeton University and Brian Shetler and Lydia Goldberg from the Princeton Theological Seminary's archives shared countless images of Mary with me for my teaching and lecturing. Rachel Fulton Brown, a medieval historian at the University of Chicago, graciously shared with me her knowledge about teaching about Mary.

A 2023–2024 sabbatical from the Princeton Theological Seminary generously supported much of the research and writing for this book. During that sabbatical, I was graciously hosted by Father Richard Finn, O.P., and Father John O'Connor, O.P., of Blackfriars Hall, Oxford University. While at Blackfriars, Lauren Spohn helped me arrange a discussion group on Mary for graduate students in theology, which ended with a half-day Marian pilgrimage. The Reverend Dr. George Westhaver, the Principal at Pusey House, Oxford, welcomed me over many teas and lunches while I was using Pusey House's excellent library for my research. I enjoyed praying the rosary with students affiliated with Pusey House and hearing about their encounters with Mary as Protestants.

The board and supporters of The Scala Foundation made it possible for me to dedicate time to this project during my sabbatical, such as through funding travel for engagements that furthered my research and writing and sponsored various webinars and interviews about Mary.

Caitrin Keiper, Lauren Spohn, Maddie Dumas, and William Gonch shared encouragement and insights on the writing in this book. Bernardine Connelly, Jeremy Wallace, and Fr. Bradley T. Elliott, O.P., each offered feedback on a few completed chapters.

Joe Durepos helped me unite my head and my heart in this project. Kathryn Riggs shared her enthusiasm for this project from the moment we connected.

My husband, David Clayton, provided unending encouragement and love during this project. His expertise in art shaped the selection of images for the book. Every day he inspires my love of Mary by chanting one or another Byzantine Marian hymn that corresponds to the time of the liturgical year commemorating different aspects of our salvation.

Author Biography

Margarita Mooney Clayton, PhD, is an Associate Professor in the Department of Practical Theology at Princeton Theological Seminary and a Research Fellow at Blackfriars Hall, Oxford University. She is also the founder of the Scala Foundation, which aims to restore meaning to American culture through beauty in the arts, education, and worship.

She earned a bachelor's degree in psychology from Yale University and a master's degree and PhD in sociology from Princeton University. She has taught in sociology programs at the University of North Carolina at Chapel Hill, Yale University, and Princeton University.

In addition to numerous academic articles, her writing has appeared in *Comment Magazine*, *America Magazine*, RealClearPolicy, *Scientific American*, *The Chronicle of Higher Education, The Hedgehog Review, Public Discourse*, *National Catholic Register*, *Plough*, *First Things*, and *Church Life Journal*. Her other published books include *Faith Makes Us Live: Surviving and Thriving in the Haitian Diaspora*, *The Love of Learning: Seven Dialogues on the Liberal Arts*, and *The Wounds of Beauty: Seven Dialogues on Art and Education*. She is a passionate keynote speaker and has lectured on beauty, education, culture, and faith at Columbia University, Harvard University, Oxford University, the

University of Notre Dame, Hillsdale College, the Consortium for Christian Studies Centers, the Acton Institute, the Society for Catholic Liturgy, and the Fellowship of Catholic Scholars.

She writes for her own online magazine called The Graced Imagination. She has been interviewed by the Acton Institute, Duke Divinity School, the University of Dallas, the Institute for Humane Studies (IHS), the American Council of Alumni and Trustees (ACTA), Mars Hill Audio with Ken Myers, *The Tammy Peterson Podcast*, and by Eric Metaxas for *Socrates in the Studio*.

She is a lifelong Catholic and attends both Roman Catholic and Byzantine Catholic parishes. She sings in the choir of The Aquinas Institute, Princeton University's Catholic Campus Ministry, under the direction of Peter Carter, the founder of The Catholic Sacred Music Project.

Notes

Introduction

1 "Evan" is a pseudonym to protect his identity.
2 James Jeffrey, "The Revival of Pilgrimage in an Age of Secularism and Distraction," *The Catholic World Report*. July 23, 2023, https://www.catholicworldreport.com/2023/07/23/the-revival-of-pilgrimage-in-an-age-of-secularism-and-distraction/
3 Matthew J. Milliner, "Everybody's Mother," *Comment*, December 4, 2023, https://comment.org/everybodys-mother/.
4 The same quote can be found in print. A.G. Dickens and Dorothy Carr, *The Reformation in England to the Ascension of Elizabeth I* (Edward Arnold Publishers, 1967), 83. See also https://www.henryviiithereign.co.uk/1538-second-injunctions.
5 K. V. Turley, "A Protestant Pilgrimage to the Marian Shrine of Walsingham," *National Catholic Register*, August 25, 2017, https://www.ncregister.com/blog/a-protestant-pilgrimage-to-the-marian-shrine-of-walsingham.
6 This quote is taken from this page of the exhibition website: "Picturing Mary: Woman, Mother, Idea," National Museum of Women in the Arts, https://nmwa.org/exhibitions/picturing-mary-woman-mother-idea/.
7 To see a description of the online exhibition, visit this link: "A Global Icon: Mary in Context," National Museum of Women in the Arts, https://nmwa.org/whats-on/exhibitions/online/global-icon/.
8 Nicholas Eberstadt, "The Age of Depopulation: Surviving a World Gone Gray," *Foreign Affairs*, October 10, 2024, https://www.foreignaffairs.com/world/age-depopulation-surviving-world-gone-gray-nicholas-eberstadt.
9 Margarita Mooney Clayton, "Why Have Children? The Global Population Decline and Human Happiness," *Public Discourse*, May 11, 2025, https://www.thepublicdiscourse.com/2025/05/97883/.

Chapter 1

1 This chapter uses pseudonyms for everyone, except for my mother.
2 Lala Suarez Mooney, *Leaving Cuba: One Family's Journey to Freedom* (Big Fox Publishing, 2019), 210.
3 Ibid., 216.
4 Pope John Paul II, "Homily of John Paul II," given in Santiago de Cuba.

The Vatican, January 24, 1998, https://www.vatican.va/content/john-paul-ii/en/homilies/1998/documents/hf_jp-ii_hom_19980124_santiago.html.

Chapter 3

1 This chapter draws on numerous private conversations with Al Raboteau, and some of his published work. When quoting his published work, those works are noted in endnotes.
2 Albert J. Raboteau, *Slave Religion, The "Invisible Institution" in the Antebellum South* (Oxford University Press, 2004), 332.
3 Ibid., 333.
4 Ibid., 331.
5 Ibid., 314.
6 Ibid., 258.
7 Albert J. Raboteau, *Sorrowful Joy: A Spiritual Journey of an African-American Man in Late Twentieth-Century America* (Wipf and Stock, 2012), 50.
8 Raboteau, *Slave Religion,* 258.
9 Ibid., 331.
10 Ibid., 334.
11 Raboteau, *Sorrowful Joy*, 51.
12 Ibid., 41.
13 Ibid.
14 Ibid., 42.
15 Ibid., 43.
16 Ibid., 56.
17 Ibid., 59.
18 Ibid., 59.
19 Ibid., 58.
20 Albert J. Raboteau, "Forgiveness and the African American Church Experience," Lecture given based on a written paper presented at The Faith Angle Forum, Miami Beach, Florida. Published online November 30, 2015, https://eppc.org/publication/dr-albert-raboteau-at-the-november-2015-faith-angle-forum/.
20 Raboteau, *Slave Religion*, 258.
21 Margarita A. Mooney. *Faith Makes Us Live: Surviving and Thriving in the Haitian Diaspora* (University of California Press, 2009), 83.
22 See my article from this event: Margarita Mooney Clayton, "Forgiving the Unforgiveable: A Lesson in Love," published online by *Public Discourse*, October 22, 2019, https://www.thepublicdiscourse.com/2019/10/57017/.
23 Parts of this section of my writing are reprinted with permission of Plough Publishing. Margarita Mooney Clayton, "Remembering a Mentor," in *The Liberating Arts: Why We Need Liberal Arts Education*, eds. Jeffrey Bilbro, Jessica Hooten Wilson, and David Henreckson (Plough Publishing, 2023), 159–162.

Chapter 4

1 Margarita Mooney, "Fátima and Perseverance in Trials," *Church Life Journal*, May 1, 2020, https://churchlifejournal.nd.edu/articles/fatima-and-perseverance-in-trials/.
2 Catechism of the Catholic Church, paragraph 494.
3 Margarita Mooney Clayton, "The Marian Gift of Dependence," published online and in print by *Comment* Magazine, September 15, 2023, https://comment.org/the-marian-gift-of-dependence/.
4 "Encyclical Letter 'Spe Salvi' of the Supreme Pontiff Pope Benedict XVI to the Bishops, Priests, Deacons, Men and Women Religious and All the Lay Faithful on Christian Hope," the Vatican, November 30, 2007, https://www.vatican.va/content/benedict-xvi/en/encyclicals/documents/hf_ben-xvi_enc_20071130_spe-salvi.html.
5 Ibid.

Chapter 5

1 In this chapter, I have provided references for published books and articles from which I draw quotes. I also quote three conversations with Aidan Hart in the text, two of which were published on YouTube, and one of which is not published. Those conversations were: 1) Aidan Hart and Margarita Mooney, "Beauty, Spirit, Matter," December 6, 2022, published on Scala's YouTube Channel; 2) Aidan Hart and Margarita Mooney Clayton, "The Annunciation and Discernment," April 22, 2023, published on Scala's YouTube channel; and 3) Aidan Hart and Margarita Mooney Clayton, "Mary and the Passion of Christ," unpublished conversation, October 29, 2024. Sections of this chapter are reprinted from: Margarita Mooney Suarez, *Introduction* to *The Wounds of Beauty: Seven Dialogues on Art and Education* (Cluny Media, 2022).
2 Aidan Hart, "Liturgical Art as Prophecy and Priesthood: Sacred Art and the Restoration of Human Dignity," unpublished talk given at the 2023 Scala Foundation Conference on Art, the Sacred and the Common Good in Princeton, NJ, p. 1. The video is available online at https://www.youtube.com/watch?v=07KxzJABskY.
3 Ibid., 4.
4 Ibid., 8.
5 Ibid., 1.
6 Ibid.
7 Jaroslav Pelikan, *Mary Through the Centuries: Her Place in the History of Culture* (Yale University Press, 1996), 36.
8 Ibid., 27.
9 Aidan Hart, *Festal Icons: History and Meaning* (Leominster, England: Gracewing, 2022), 22.
10 Ibid., ix.
11 Ibid., 15.

Chapter 6

1 James MacMillan, "God, Theology and Music," *New Blackfriars* 81, no. 947 (2000): 21.
2 This chapter draws on several conversations between me and James MacMillan and some of his published work. When quoting his published work, those works are noted in the endnotes. The one published conversation I draw from "Silence and Music: A Scotsman's Song" that is on YouTube was published on July 26, 2024, and can be seen here: https://www.youtube.com/watch?v=Gexj7JEVeS8&t=63s.
3 MacMillan, "God, Theology and Music," 18.
4 Ibid.
5 Ibid.
6 Ibid., 20.
7 Ibid., 19.
8 Ibid., 20–21.
9 Ibid., 22.
10 Ibid.
11 Ibid., 23.
12 Ibid., 24.
13 James MacMillan, *A Scots Song: A Life of Music* (Birlinn Limited, 2019), 86.
14 Ibid.
15 Caryll Houselander, *The Reed of God* (Christian Classics, 2006), 73.
16 Jacques Maritain, *Creative Intuition in Art and Poetry*, with an Introduction by Raymond Hain (Cluny Media, 2018), 131.
17 Ibid., 173.
18 Pope John Paul II, "Letter of His Holiness Pope John Paull II to Artists," the Vatican, 1999, https://www.vatican.va/content/john-paul-ii/en/letters/1999/documents/hf_jp-ii_let_23041999_artists.html.
19 James MacMillan, "The Most Spiritual of the Arts: Music, Modernity and the Search for the Sacred," in *Annunciations: Sacred Music for the Twenty-First Century*, ed. George Corbett (Open Book Publishers, 2019), 16.
20 Ibid.
21 Ibid.
22 These recordings are available only to subscribers to the BBC at this location: https://www.bbc.co.uk/programmes/b006tnvx.
23 MacMillan, "God, Theology and Music," 26.

Chapter 7

1 Quotations in this chapter are taken from many private conversations with Tammy Peterson and two recorded conversations published on Tammy's podcast. See "Finding Mary: The Role of Women in the Church," recorded on July 16, 2024, https://sites.libsyn.com/409622/107-finding-mary-the-role-of-women-in-the-church-margarita-mooney-clayton 2; "Miracles, Mary and Modern Faith," August 15, 2024, https://sites.libsyn.com/409622/108-miracles-mary-and-modern-faith-margarita-mooney-clayton.

2 Aidan Nichols, *Lessons in a Rose-Garden: Reviving the Doctrinal Rosary* (Gracewing, 2012), 2.

Conclusion

1 This resource can be accessed online via Open Athens. https://pm-nlx-com.eu1.proxy.openathens.net/xtf/view?docId=calvin/calvin.07.xml;chunk.id=div.calvin.letters.2.171;toc.depth=1;toc.id=div.calvin.letters.2.14;brand=default.

2 This resource can be accessed online via Open Athens. https://pm-nlx-com.eu1.proxy.openathens.net/xtf/view?docId=luther_w/luther_w.21.xml;chunk.id=div.CH2;toc.depth=1;toc.id=div.CH2;brand=default

3 This document can be accessed online at this link. https://iarccum.org/doc/16.